Happiness, Health, and Beauty

*W*esleyan Doctrine Series

The Wesleyan Doctrine Series seeks to reintroduce Christians in the Wesleyan tradition to the beauty of doctrine. The volumes in the series draw on the key sources for Wesleyan teaching: Scripture, Liturgy, Hymnody, the General Rules, the Articles of Religion and various Confessions. In this sense, it seeks to be distinctively Wesleyan. But it does this with a profound interest and respect for the unity and catholicity of Christ's body, the church, which is also distinctly Wesleyan. For this reason, the series supplements the Wesleyan tradition with the gifts of the church catholic, ancient, and contemporary. The Wesleyan tradition cannot survive without a genuine "Catholic Spirit." These volumes are intended for laity who have a holy desire to understand the faith they received at their baptism.

EDITORS:
Randy Cooper
Andrew Kinsey
D. Brent Laytham
D. Stephen Long

Happiness, Health, and Beauty

The Christian Life in Everyday Terms

DEBRA DEAN MURPHY

With Questions for Consideration by Andrew Kinsey

CASCADE *Books* · Eugene, Oregon

HAPPINESS, HEALTH, AND BEAUTY
The Christian Life in Everyday Terms

Wesleyan Doctrine Series 9

Cascade Books
An Imprint of Wipf and Stock Publishers
199 W. 8th Ave., Suite 3
Eugene, OR 97401

www.wipfandstock.com

ISBN 13: 978-1-62032-511-7

Cataloging-in-Publication data:

Murphy, Debra Dean, 1962–

   Happiness, health, and beauty : the Christian life in everyday terms / Debra Dean Murphy ; with Andrew Kinsey.

   xii + 98 p. ; 23 cm. —Includes bibliographical references.

   Wesleyan Doctrine Series 9

   ISBN 13: 978-1-62032-511-7

   1. Happiness—Religious aspects—Christianity. 2. Health—Religious aspects—Christianity. 3. Aesthetics—Religious aspects—Christianity. 4. Wesley, John, 1703–1791. 5. Wesley, Charles, 1707–1788. I. Kinsey, Andrew. II. Title. III. Series.

BV4647.J68 M87 2015

Manufactured in the U.S.A.

For the community of St. Meinrad Archabbey in Indiana,
whose gifts of hospitality and the daily rhythm of prayer and work
made the writing of this book possible.

Contents

Introduction

This is "The Christian Life" volume in the Wesleyan Doctrine Series. Unlike, perhaps, "The Trinity" or "The Sacraments" (other subjects in the series) there is considerable discretion in determining what might count for content in such a book. Should we think of the Christian life primarily as a matter of ethics: how it is we seek, embrace, and embody the good? Or is it better understood in terms of formation and transformation: how we learn over time the way of Jesus? Or perhaps it is fundamentally about bearing witness: how we manifest the love of God and neighbor in all that we do. The Christian life is, of course, all of these and more. And each of these ways of naming and describing it is deeply entangled in the others. Ethics, for example, cannot be separated from the shape (and the shaping) of our lives, and learning and living the way of Jesus *is* the witness we make in the world, both personally and corporately.

Because this series is about *doctrine*, this volume takes note of the church's historic teaching in three areas: personhood, salvation, and Christian perfection. More narrowly, since these are thick subjects beyond the scope of so slim a treatment, the guiding tropes for our inquiry into the nature of the Christian life and its rootedness in classic Christian doctrine are these: *happiness* (what humans are created for), *health* (the well-being made possible in Christ), and *beauty* (what lies at the center of the pursuit of perfection). Moreover, this book series draws on key sources in Wesleyan theology (sermons, hymns, etc.), while also putting those sources in conversation with the wider Christian tradition. To that end, this volume on the Christian life reads the Wesleys (John and Charles) alongside several other writers—theologians, philosophers, social critics, scientists, and poets—ancient, medieval, and contemporary.

⤙⤚

Chapter 1 begins by examining the idea of *happiness* as it is culturally and theologically understood, and notes that both advertisers and careful readers of Scripture share a similar conviction about the nature of being human—that we are created for happiness. Yet there is this fundamental difference: where consumerism would have us believe that happiness is seized (or made, or merited) by the individual, the Christian tradition has always maintained that genuine happiness is a gift that comes as goodness is desired, sought, and practiced in relationship with others. The first chapter also looks at some common approaches to the Beatitudes, Jesus' description of blessedness or happiness that opens the lengthy discourse in Matthew's Gospel known as the Sermon on the Mount (*Beātitûdō = perfect happiness*). The tendencies to personalize, sentimentalize, and deem impossible Jesus' words in the Sermon are treated in turn; then John Wesley's reading of the Beatitudes is examined. Drawing on sources both Protestant and Catholic, the attempt here is to suggest how the Christian life is a reimagining, over and against certain cultural construals, of what counts as genuine happiness. Assuming that Jesus' words in the Sermon refer to life lived in community with and for others, this chapter also seeks to show how the Beatitudes cannot be understood apart from what it means to be members of Christ's body, recipients and bearers of the promises of a good and generous God.

Chapter 2 links physical health with Holy Communion. It looks at how Scripture equates salvation with the health and well-being of bodies, minds, spirits, and communities, and it examines the eucharistic theology of John and Charles Wesley in light of current global health crises. The Christian life lived eucharistically acknowledges that all our sharing of food (and our withholding or wasting of it), our complicity with unjust food systems, and, perhaps most unsettling, all our eating (and overeating) are challenged by our participation in the Eucharist—the church's signature feast in which we consume the body of Christ in order to become the body of Christ for a hungry, ill-fed world.

Chapter 3 explores the concept of beauty in contemporary culture and in theological discourse. The Protestant Reformation laid the groundwork for generations of Christians to be suspicious of beauty—in life, in art, in church, especially. In many ways, early Methodist theology followed this path. But the Wesleyan doctrine of perfection offers a way to name and locate beauty within lived discipleship, within the practices of the love of

God and neighbor that constitute the sum of the Christian life. Beauty, we will see, reveals itself as a disposition to benevolence, as an active seeking of the well-being of all that exists, and thus beauty is intrinsically connected to happiness and health. The Christian stance toward beauty, then, is not fundamentally a utilitarian one (how should we make use of beautiful objects and experiences or how are we to *appreciate* beauty). Rather, our task is to practice the humble, gentle, patient love of God and neighbor, and thus put ourselves in the way of the gift of becoming beautiful.

Comments

Debra Dean Murphy's commentary on happiness, health, and beauty provides an excellent opportunity to explore these sometimes misunderstood and neglected teachings in the life of the church. Putting Wesleyan themes and practices in conversation with the wider Christian tradition she highlights the significance of these concepts in communal terms, noting how they are relentlessly social and political. The work she has done offers a helpful glimpse into the richness of what happiness, health, and beauty entail in our life together in Christ.

The following Questions for Consideration have been created to guide persons and groups into the issues Murphy raises. While they do not in any way exhaust all the angles, they will hopefully stimulate further discussion, perhaps action, about what it means to "become like God in goodness." Murphy's commentary is one of several commentaries in the Wesleyan Doctrine Series designed to engage the church in ongoing spiritual formation and instruction.

Andrew Kinsey

one

Happiness: The Christian Life and the Human Calling

Happiness is fundamentally an activity; it is the state of the person who is living without hindrance the life that becomes a human being.

—Herbert McCabe, *The Good Life*

The sum of all true religion is laid down in eight particulars ...

—John Wesley, "Upon Our Lord's Sermon on the Mount, Discourse I"

Blessed are the poor in spirit, for theirs is the kingdom of heaven.
Blessed are those who mourn, for they will be comforted.
Blessed are the meek, for they will inherit the earth.
Blessed are those who hunger and thirst for righteousness,
    for they will be filled.
Blessed are the merciful, for they will receive mercy.
Blessed are the pure in heart, for they will see God.
Blessed are the peacemakers, for they will be called children of God.
Blessed are those who are persecuted for righteousness' sake,
    for theirs is the kingdom of heaven.

—Matt 5:3–10

Being Human, Being Happy

Popular advertising slogans could lead a person to think that happiness is what human beings are made for. Coca-Cola invites us to "open happiness." At the International House of Pancakes it is "come hungry, leave happy," while the all-you-can-eat restaurant chain Golden Corral entreats, "help yourself to happiness." Disneyland, since the mid-1960s, boasts that it is "the happiest place on earth." We feed children "happy meals," strive for a "happy medium," admire the "happy-go-lucky" (who seem to live by the mantra "don't worry, be happy")—all while trying to find our own private "happy place." Even one of our nation's founding documents, the Declaration of Independence, asserts that human beings have an "unalienable right" to the "pursuit of happiness." Happiness, it seems, is ever on our minds (and on our stomachs, if the corporate restaurateurs are to be believed). We want desperately to be happy.

But what counts as genuine happiness? If, as corporations like Coca-Cola and Disney would have us believe, happiness can be had in the products and experiences we consume, why are we—the savviest shoppers in the history of modern advertising—notoriously *un*happy?[1] At least one answer to this question can be found in poet John Ciardi's observation, made half a century ago, that advertising and the whole of our economy are based on "dedicated insatiability."[2] It isn't that consumerism makes us happy by satisfying our desires for material goods or attractively packaged experiences; rather, our consumer culture trains us to be perpetually *dissatisfied*. As theologian William Cavanaugh has observed, consumerism is not so much about having *more* as it is about having *something else*.[3] So the happiness I might feel at acquiring a new pair of shoes or a luxury vacation (increased, perhaps, if I believe I got a good deal on the purchase) is not only a kind of temporary pleasure since soon enough the newness of the product or the experience will fade and my euphoria with it. Rather, American consumer culture teaches me that the pleasure of consumption is itself *in the very process of acquiring* my good deal: advertisers want me, want all of us, to be addicted not to things but to the endless pursuit of things. And most of us seem all too happy to oblige.

1. See the Harris Poll Happiness Index: http://www.harrisinteractive.com/News-Room/HarrisPolls/tabid/447/ctl/ReadCustom%20Default/mid/1508/ArticleId/1200/Default.aspx.

2. Ciardi, "Is Everybody Happy?," 18.

3. Cavanaugh, *Being Consumed*, 35.

Yet even if we concede that the happiness held out by marketing campaigns is fleeting if not false, shallow, and ultimately unsatisfying, why do we still find ourselves seduced by the promise that happiness can be ours if only we secure the ideal job or find the perfect mate, if we just lose those excess pounds or raise successful children or earn the respect of our peers? Perhaps this promise lures us because a hunger for happiness is at the heart of what it means to be human. As theologian Paul Wadell observes, "The story of our lives can be read as one unfolding search for happiness because we relentlessly pursue whatever we think will be good for us; whatever we suspect will fulfill us, delight us, bring us peace, and deepen the meaning of our lives."[4]

The Christian tradition has always held that human beings are created for happiness, but it has defined ultimate happiness as knowing, loving, and enjoying God. We are created in the image of God, bearing something of the divine within us, and thus communion with our Creator—and with all of creation—is central to what it means to be fully human. Famously, St. Augustine declared that our hearts are restless till they find rest in God. The Westminster Catechism opens by asking what is the purpose of our lives as human beings, and answering with this: to love God and to enjoy God forever. And St. Thomas Aquinas, in perhaps one of the most thorough treatments of the subject, observed that happiness is intimately linked with goodness. In this he was following Aristotle, who believed that only goodness can make us happy. And while there are many goods intrinsic to a life of happiness—food, shelter, satisfying work to do, enough money to live on, art and music and beauty of all kinds to stir our imaginations, friends and loved ones to enjoy all of these things with—the highest good and our ultimate happiness can be found, Aquinas believed, only in God.

Happiness as Gift-in-Community

But how does that work exactly? What would it *look* like to discover and experience complete happiness in God? For Aquinas, attaining ultimate happiness is a matter of our becoming like God in goodness. But this, too, sounds far-fetched—impossible, even (and perhaps not a little presumptuous). How can we become like God in anything?

In contrast to a culture that trains us to view happiness as something we buy or take or make, something we earn or deserve or accomplish, the

4. Wadell, *Happiness and the Christian Moral Life*, 2.

Christian tradition has insisted that a life of genuine happiness is beyond our own powers and capacities. It is not, as much talk-show psychology would have it, something available within us if only we would reach down deep enough to find it. Rather, genuine happiness comes to us through grace; it is a gift. "The God who wants our good," Wadell says, "gifts us with the happiness we seek."[5] Our lifelong task, then, to repurpose a beautiful phrase from novelist Marilynne Robinson, is to put ourselves in the way of the gift.[6]

The happiness we were made for, that comes to us as gift to be received rather than goal to be achieved (or interior state to be accessed), is, as Scripture makes clear, relentlessly *social*. This is at least one reason why seeking happiness through the exercise of individual choice in a market economy is a futile quest. In the opening chapters of Genesis we learn that God created human beings for friendship with one another and with God, and the book of Revelation describes powerfully the heavenly communion that characterizes the ultimate happiness—the beatific vision—for which all of creation is destined. Thus the Bible reveals, from beginning to end, that the gift of happiness is deeply social, "ineluctably political."[7] "Political," in this sense, has to do with how human beings are constituted by community and how we might flourish in it—how it is that we are good *together*. There is no human thriving, no genuine happiness apart from life lived in connection with others as the good is sought and practiced and enjoyed and witnessed to. For Aristotle, this meant that the *polis* is "more than a pact of mutual protection or an agreement to exchange goods and services. . . . [It] is intended to enable all, in their households and their kinships, to live *well*."[8] In Christian terms we would say that through the sacrament of Baptism we are initiated into a *polis*—the communion of saints being one way to name it—and that in the Eucharist we are nourished and sustained as a community of friends who, week after week, year after year, enact our desire to be transformed into the likeness of Christ, to be drawn more and more deeply into the goodness of God. Yet even in the *polis* of the worshiping community, our attempts to "become like God in goodness" are not our own moral achievements. As we have said, all of this comes through grace and as gift.

5. Ibid., 16.

6. Robinson, *Gilead*, 134.

7. McCabe, *Good Life*, 25.

8. Aristotle, *Politics*, III, 9, quoted in McCabe, *Good Life*, 38. Italics McCabe's.

This too is borne out in Scripture. When God calls the people of Israel into covenant relationship, God gives them all that they need to flourish: food and land and work and words to live by. The Decalogue given to the people at Mount Sinai is not a dreary list of prohibitions, disembodied regulations meant to govern personal morality so that those who adhere to them will earn God's favor and escape his wrath. We forget sometimes that the law comes *after* Israel's salvation and in response to it, not as a precondition of it. Rather, the "ten words" name the parameters and conditions of life in a particular *polis*—the covenant community of Israel—so that the people of God might be good together, that they might learn how to put themselves in the way of the gift of happiness and fullness of life.

Jesus and the Goodness of God

In the New Testament Jesus himself is the Word (*Logos*) who embodies fully the goodness of God. He heals the sick, feeds the hungry, eats with sinners. He prays, teaches, blesses, and forgives. He preaches the kingdom of God not as a matter of geography (the hoped-for, far-off place we go to when we die) but as a living rule of love, mercy, and generosity in this and every age. When he washes his disciples' feet the night before his death he reveals the way of the kingdom as servanthood and humility. When he refuses to meet the brutality brought against him with vengeance and violence, he establishes peaceableness as his way in the world. In his resurrection the church finds its hope. In Jesus we do not have to wonder what God is like, what God's goodness entails. Again and again, in word and deed, in his actions and interactions, Jesus shows us the heart of God.

When Jesus speaks of happiness, as he does in the Sermon on the Mount in Matthew's Gospel, he does many things. He upsets expectations, not surprisingly, as to what counts as genuine happiness. He makes clear that his own life is an embodiment of the blessedness (happiness) he names—what he enjoins on his followers he makes manifest in himself. And he bears witness to the continuity between Israel and the Church, to God's faithfulness in giving to all of God's people everything they need in order to become like God in goodness—to flourish in genuine happiness.

The Gospel of Matthew makes this latter point evident by having Jesus offer his words from atop a mountain (Matt 5:1).[9] For Matthew, a

9. Luke, by contrast, has Jesus preaching a version of this sermon on level ground (6:17–49). His Gospel has a special concern for the poor and marginalized and words of

Jew writing to Jewish followers of Jesus, the setting itself deliberately calls to mind the giving of the law upon Mount Sinai. Jesus, the new Moses, ascends the mountain and draws his disciples to him; he *is* the promised, long-awaited Messiah of Israel. For its original hearers, this sermon is delivered by God's own Son, who calls the people of Israel to the fullness of their life in God and who—in his very being, his living and dying and being raised from death—inaugurates a new community, a new ordering of human relationships. As the *Logos* made flesh, what this Messiah says cannot be separated from who he is. Twentieth-century German theologian Dietrich Bonhoeffer put it this way: "The Sermon on the Mount is the word of the very one who is the lord and law of reality. The Sermon on the Mount is to be understood and interpreted as the word of the God who became human."[10]

Personal, Sentimental, Impossible

The words that Jesus speaks from the mountaintop are familiar. Perhaps they are too familiar to do the work they are intended to do in the people— the *polis*, the Church—to whom and for whom they were given. As with the Ten Commandments, the Beatitudes have often been taken as general principles for the individual to live by—rules for getting into heaven or getting along well with others, for being a good citizen or a decent person. We see the familiar words of the Sermon printed on inspirational posters and cross-stitched onto homey samplers. We may have read self-help books or heard well-meaning sermons or homilies interpreting the Beatitudes as keys for successful living or inner peace. But, as we will see, who Jesus blesses in these "eight particulars" reveals a *community's* way of life, not a prescription for individual self-actualization. Moreover, what Jesus blesses are not moral states he orders his followers to achieve—be meek! be peacemakers!—but the conditions of our shared life as we seek to flourish together in the goodness of God. And, as we have indicated already, if happiness is a *political* reality—the flourishing we experience as we seek to practice the goodness of God together—all that Jesus says in the Beatitudes (indeed, in the Sermon in its entirety) must be understood as an invitation

---

warning for the rich. One Lukan commentary describes this as "the boundary-breaking ministry of Jesus." Bartholomew et al., *Reading Luke*, 246.

10. Bonhoeffer, *Ethics*, 231.

to particular forms of behavior that bind us in love and responsibility to one another.

If Christians have been tempted toward individualism and sentimentality when it comes to the Beatitudes, we have also imagined these sayings of Jesus to be admirable but impossible ideals. According to such a view, what Jesus blesses at the beginning of the Sermon serves primarily as a set of reminders of our need for grace in failing to measure up to the high standards of the Christian life. So, for instance, meekness ("blessed are the meek," Matt 5:5) has often been understood as a commendable but ultimately unrealistic character trait—part of an impossible ethic—in the world in which we live. Being meek in a culture of frenetic competition and scarcity (of jobs, say) is simply a losing life strategy. We might admire this quality in people we think of as super-devout—a pastor or priest or saintly grandmother—but for most of us, all we can do is acknowledge the impossibility, even the inadvisability, of practicing meekness.

In fact, interpreting the Beatitudes and the Sermon itself through the lens of "the world in which we live" is why these pronouncements have often been deemed impossible ideals. According to this view, we live in a world of danger and great evil; in many situations, meekness would be a form of recklessness or irresponsibility. And "blessed are the peacemakers"? We all want peace, of course, but—regrettably—force is often necessary to achieve it. That's just the world we live in. So goes this logic.

Beginning in the 1930s, Protestant moral theologian Reinhold Niebuhr argued for a method of interpreting the Sermon on the Mount— and indeed all of Scripture—that takes as its starting point the dangerous, fallen world we live in. Over his long career, with two world wars and the horrors of the Holocaust informing his theological conclusions on a range of subjects, Niebuhr insisted that Christians must be realistic about the nature of sin and radical evil in the world. He took the Sermon on the Mount seriously; he was not dismissive or derisive of its substantive claims. But for Niebuhr, the Sermon consisted of a series of "ethical demands" (a characterization under scrutiny here) that can be fulfilled only when the kingdom of God is fully realized.[11] In the present age, Niebuhr insisted, Jesus's ethic of love "does not deal at all with the immediate moral problem of every human life—the problem of arranging some kind of armistice between

---

11. Niebuhr, *Interpretation of Christian Ethics*, 35.

various contending factions and forces. . . . It has only a vertical dimension between the loving will of God and the will of man."[12]

Niebuhr's views, even for Christians who may have never heard of him, have exerted a powerful influence on contemporary readings of the Sermon on the Mount. Because he was persuasive in articulating a biblical hermeneutic that begins with "the way the world is"—that is, because he thought that Scripture's claims must be evaluated first and foremost in light of the exigencies of a fallen world—many Christians in the generations since have too readily assumed that "representative democracy" names an ordering of social relations more foundational than "the body of Christ." Since many if not most expressions of contemporary American Christianity (Protestant and Catholic, liberal and conservative, high church and low) are heirs to the realism represented by Reinhold Niebuhr, "any talk of the church as holy or as a paradigmatic community of witness or as having its own politics is problematic."[13]

In contrast to Niebuhr's Christian realism with its unquestioning deference to "the facts of a given situation," there exists a longstanding tradition we have begun to sketch already: that the Church itself is a social body (*polis*) whose end (*telos*) is the flourishing of all creation in the goodness of God. According to this view, the Sermon on the Mount is not a list of impossible demands intended for the individual Christian's personal faith but a description of and a summons to a communal way of life—the way of ultimate blessedness or happiness. The Sermon is an invitation to a way of life that does not originate in abstract principles or disembodied ethical mandates but in the one who issues the invitation for us to come and see what it might look like to be good together, to share in the fullness of life and love that glimpses the goodness of God.

"The Whole Plan of His Religion"

In eighteenth-century England, a churchman named John Wesley saw in the Sermon on the Mount "the full prospect" of the Christian life.[14] He devoted thirteen discourses—dense, lengthy treatises—to the Sermon and between 1739 and 1746 preached more than one hundred sermons on various

12. Ibid., 23.

13. Bretherton, *Christianity and Contemporary Politics*, 90.

14. Wesley, "Upon Our Lord's Sermon on the Mount, Discourse I" (hereafter "Sermon on the Mount, I"), in Wesley, *Works*, 1:473.

portions of it. According to theologian and historian Albert Outler, Wesley detected a threefold pattern of themes in the design of Matthew 5–7:

1. the sum of true religion;
2. rules touching that right intention which we are to preserve in all our outward actions; and
3. the main hindrances of this religion.[15]

The first of these refers only to the Beatitudes. Wesley sees in them the entirety of Jesus's teaching and marvels that in no other place in the New Testament do we have "heavenly wisdom" to this degree, nor a description of "the nature of that holiness without which no [one] shall see God."[16] Moreover, Wesley saw laid out in the whole of chapter 5 those dispositions, affections, patterns of behavior, and forms of excellence that "constitute real Christianity."[17] In the second theme Wesley notes the cautionary norms necessary for keeping the actions enjoined in the Sermon "unmixed with worldly desires, or anxious cares for even the necessaries of life."[18] In chapter 6 of Matthew Jesus offers particular injunctions regarding almsgiving, prayer, and fasting in order that these practices might be true and devoid of hypocrisy: "whenever you give alms, do not sound a trumpet before you" (6:2); "when you are praying, do not heap up empty phrases as the Gentiles do" (6:7); and "whenever you fast, do not look dismal" (6:16). For Wesley, engaging in these acts of piety without a holiness of intention "is of no value before God."[19] The third theme that Wesley detects in the Sermon on the Mount unfolds in two ways. Outler notes that in the first part of chapter 7 (vv. 1–12) Wesley identifies the fatal hindrances to the holiness that characterizes the Christian way of life: judging others, intemperate zeal, the neglect of prayer, and the failure of charity. And in the latter part of the chapter, he observes, Jesus "exhorts us, by various motives, to break through all [such hindrances] and secure that prize of our high calling."[20] This breaking through occurs when followers of Jesus imitate the wise man and build their houses on rock instead of sand (7:24–27).

15. Ibid., 467.
16. Ibid., 474.
17. Ibid.
18. Ibid., 474–75.
19. Ibid., 573.
20. Ibid., 468.

After mapping chapters 5 through 7 in this way, Wesley returns to the Beatitudes in the thirteenth discourse, where he notes that the states of blessedness that constitute "inward and outward holiness" produce persons who, for instance, in their own mourning, "weep with them that weep" and who, in practicing meekness, avoid "every inward emotion contrary to love."[21] For Wesley, those whom Jesus calls "blessed" (or as he says in the first discourse, "*happy*—so the word should be rendered") *do* and *undergo* certain things: "Be thou a lover of God and of all mankind. In this spirit do and suffer all things."[22] Dominican theologian Herbert McCabe's insight is fitting here: "Happiness is fundamentally an activity; it is the state of the person who is living without hindrance the life that becomes a human being."[23]

Before we look at each of the Beatitudes in turn, it is helpful to note that for Wesley and for most interpreters through the centuries, the first ten verses of Matthew 5 hang together as a cohesive unit. Like a tapestry thread or a shard of mosaic glass, no single "blessed are" can be separated from the whole. Fifth-century theologian Gregory of Nyssa likened the Beatitudes to rungs on a ladder leading to union with God, with each ascending step building on and surpassing what comes before it.[24] There may be difficulties with such a metaphor (Gregory has to do some creative interpreting to make the ladder analogy work with the order and progression of the verses themselves), but he is persuasive in his insistence on the unity and interdependence of the Beatitudes themselves.

We also remember here something noted earlier (but which is not always evident in Wesley's reading of the Sermon): the Beatitudes are not separate from the one who speaks them. For instance, we can know what being merciful is only by looking intently at the life of Jesus. Another early church theologian, Origen of Alexandria, states it eloquently:

> Jesus confirms all of the beatitudes he speaks in the Gospel, and he justifies his teaching through his own example. "Blessed are the meek" is what he says of himself. "Learn of me, for I am meek." "Blessed are the peacemakers." Who is a peacemaker like my Lord Jesus, who is our peace, who made enmity to cease and destroyed it in his flesh? "Blessed are they who suffer persecution

21. Ibid., 696–97.
22. Ibid., 698.
23. McCabe, *Good Life*, 7.
24. Gregory of Nyssa, *Homilies on the Beatitudes*, 18.

for righteousness' sake." No one more than the Lord Jesus, who was crucified for our sins, endured persecution for righteousness' sake. The Lord, then, displays all the beatitudes as being realized in himself. Conforming to that which he said, "Blessed are those who weep," he himself wept over Jerusalem, to lay the foundation of this beatitude also.[25]

Putting it in more contemporary terms, United Methodist pastor James Howell says that "when reading the Beatitudes, we may overhear something of an autobiographical reflection, as if Jesus is saying in a subtext, 'This is who I am, and so this is what friendship with me looks like, for this is what oneness with God looks like.'"[26]

The Poor in Spirit and Those Who Mourn

"Blessed are the poor in spirit, for theirs is the kingdom of heaven."

In his first discourse on the first of the Beatitudes, Wesley does not make reference to Luke's version, in which Jesus says only, "Blessed are the poor" (Luke 6:20). But it is an interesting contrast with Matthew's Sermon. Knowing that the materially impoverished, the destitute poor, the chronically deprived would have constituted the majority of Jesus's day-to-day followers—the crowds who pressed in on him and who, we might suppose, created the occasion for him to ascend the mountain to preach—Matthew's wording is noteworthy. For our purposes it is instructive to consider how this difference is perceived in our culture of material abundance, in which the disparity between rich and poor is striking and ever-widening. Clarence Jordan, the founder of Koinonia Farm, a community of blacks and whites who began living and working together in rural Georgia in the 1940s, said this on the question of whether Jesus intended physical or spiritual poverty:

> If you have a lot of money, you'll probably say spiritual poverty. If you have little or no money, you'll probably say physical poverty. The rich will thank God for Matthew; the poor will thank God for Luke. Who's right? Chances are, neither one. For it is exactly this attitude of self-praise and self-justification and self-satisfaction that robs [people] of a sense of great need for the kingdom and its blessings. When one says, "I don't need to be poor in things; I'm

25. Origen, *Homilies on St. Luke*, 38.1–2, quoted in Allison, *Studies in Matthew*, 150.
26. Howell, *Beatitudes for Today*, 23.

poor in spirit," and another says, "I don't need to be poor in spirit; I'm poor in things," both are justifying themselves as they are, and are saying in unison, "I don't need." With that cry on [the] lips, no [one] can repent.[27]

Wesley does treat the idea that "the poor in spirit" might be those who seek material poverty, but he rejects this interpretation for three reasons. First, because he thinks it is based on a misreading of 1 Tim 6:10, translated in Wesley's day as "the love of money is the root of all evil." The New Revised Standard Version renders the verse this way: "The love of money is a root of all kinds of evil." This is the sense of the text that Wesley was keen to promote: "there are a thousand other roots of evil in the world, as sad experience daily shows."[28] Second, Wesley argued that to equate the "the poor in spirit" with those who embrace material poverty would "by no means suit our Lord's present design, which is to lay a general foundation whereon the whole fabric of Christianity may be built; a design which would be in no wise answered by guarding against one particular vice."[29] And, third, for Wesley, if poverty of spirit is synonymous with freedom from covetousness or from the desire for riches, we would have to charge Jesus with a "manifest tautology," since such traits are constitutive of what he means later in the Beatitudes by "purity of heart."[30] What Wesley does say is that poverty of spirit is "the first step toward all real, substantial happiness, either in this world or in that which is to come."[31] Here he takes Jesus to mean that happy are those who are fully convinced of their "utter sinfulness, guilt, and helplessness."[32] This way of interpreting the first Beatitude is in keeping with the character of Wesley's anthropology—his belief that "all human

---

27. Jordan, *Sermon on the Mount*, 20, quoted in Howell, *Beatitudes for Today*, 35–36.

28. Wesley, "Sermon on the Mount, Discourse I," in Wesley, *Works*, 1:476.

29. Ibid.

30. Wesley's anti-Catholicism (typical of the Anglicanism of his era) reveals itself here when he says that this identification of "poverty of spirit" with the embrace of physical poverty has caused many to wholly divest themselves not only of money but of worldly goods. "Hence," he says, "the vows of voluntary poverty seem to have arisen in the Romish Church; it being supposed that so eminent a degree of this fundamental grace must be a large step toward the kingdom of heaven" ("Sermon on the Mount, Discourse I," in Wesley, *Works*, 1:476). With some unintended irony, Wesley warns against the "danger of riches" in Discourse VIII, and increasingly throughout his life embraced and enjoined voluntary poverty as a means of mitigating the dangers of wealth.

31. Wesley, "Sermon on the Mount, Discourse I," in Wesley, *Works*, 1:476.

32. Ibid., 480.

beings come into the world already separate from God, hence spiritually dead."[33] Sin, for Wesley, is talked about in both therapeutic and juridical terms—that is, as both sickness and offense. And both are evident in his discussion of the first Beatitude. But happiness is found, he contends, when our poverty of spirit leads us to "a continual sense of our total dependence on him for every good thought or word or work; of our utter inability to all good unless he 'water us every moment' [cf. Isa 27:3]."[34] For Wesley, contra Origen, Jesus is not the exemplar of the poverty of spirit he calls us to; rather, he is the cure for the sin-sickness that ails us all.

In his theological commentary on Matthew's Gospel, Stanley Hauerwas uses St. Paul to show that "it is from Jesus that we learn what it means to be 'poor in spirit.'"[35] The well-known hymn from the Letter to the Philippians describes Jesus's emptying of self and enjoins the same on all who would follow Christ:

> Let the same mind be in you that was in Christ Jesus,
> who, though he was in the form of God,
> did not regard equality with God
> as something to be exploited,
> but emptied himself,
> taking the form of a slave,
> being born in human likeness.
> And being found in human form,
> he humbled himself
> and became obedient to the point of death—
> even death on a cross. (Phil 2:5–8)

For those who humble themselves in imitation of the self-emptying love of Christ Jesus, theirs is the kingdom of heaven. As noted earlier, when Jesus uses the phrase "kingdom of heaven" he does not so much mean reward in the afterlife as a share in the reign of God's reconciling love in the here and now. The kingdom of heaven is an *eschatological* reality in the teaching of Jesus; it is the not-yet-fully-realized wholeness and well-being that God desires for all of creation. Repeatedly in the gospels Jesus tells his followers that the kingdom of God (or heaven, in Matthew) is near. It is near because

---

33. Maddox, *Responsible Grace*, 81.

34. Wesley, "Sermon on the Mount, Discourse I," in Wesley, *Works*, 1:482.

35. Hauerwas, *Matthew*, 64.

Jesus is in their midst—he is the perfect embodiment of God's *shalom*. And it is near when people put into practice the way of Jesus, the way of God's *shalom*: when we forgive, the kingdom is near; when we practice patience, hospitality, and humility, the kingdom is near. And in the first of the Beatitudes Jesus promises that the poor in spirit—those who imitate his self-emptying love—will be heirs and bearers of such a kingdom.

There is another possibility. New Testament scholar Frederick Dale Bruner suggests that Matthew's and Luke's version of the first Beatitude are not so far apart after all. Whereas in Luke Jesus says, "Blessed are the poor," Matthew renders into Greek what Jesus originally said in Aramaic, which is in keeping with the Hebrew word for the materially poor (*'anawim*), "namely, those who are poor and feel crushed as a result."[36] What Jesus means, says Bruner, is "'blessed are those who *feel* their poverty,' we may even say, 'who *suffer* their poverty,' and so cry out."[37]

One of Jesus's familiar parables can perhaps help flesh out this richly layered notion of poverty of spirit and also allow us to underscore Wesley's important insight about this state of blessedness having to do with total dependence on God and others. In the story of the prodigal son (Luke 15:11–32), the wasteful, washed-up second son, having squandered every gift he'd been generously given, returns home empty, exhausted, broke, and broken. His dutiful older brother is angry and resentful. But his father welcomes the boy with relief and gratitude, with lavish celebration, and with unasked-for forgiveness. As many commentators have noted, it is really the father who is the prodigal in this story: the one who is wastefully extravagant—reckless in his generosity, forgiveness, and love. The son who returns to his father is poor in spirit. He *feels* his material lack, is crushed by it. And he has also surrendered everything, emptied himself of all pride and pretense ("taking the form of a slave"), and in his poverty finds the riches of welcome and blessing and home.

In his book *The Return of the Prodigal Son*, Catholic priest and author Henri Nouwen says, "The Beatitudes offer me the simplest route for the journey home. . . . And as I reach home and feel the embrace of my Father, I will realize that not only heaven will be mine to claim, but that the earth as well will become my inheritance, a place where I can live in freedom without obsessions and compulsions."[38] Nouwen also sees in this parable

---

36. Bruner, *Matthew*, 159.

37. Ibid.

38. Nouwen, *Return of the Prodigal Son*, 54.

the "mystery" that Jesus becomes the prodigal son for our sake. Leaving the home of his Father, he travels to a foreign country, is stripped of everything he has, and returns by way of the cross to his Father's home. "Jesus is the prodigal son of the prodigal Father," says Nouwen, "who gave away every-thing the Father had entrusted to him so that I could become like him and return with him to his Father's home."[39]

↤

If Jesus is describing in the Beatitudes what happiness looks like, and if ultimate happiness, as we noted earlier, is knowing, loving, and enjoying God—learning to be like God in goodness—then perhaps we can also say that to be happy is to be at home in the generous communion of the triune God who loves patiently, extravagantly, recklessly. And just as in the story of the prodigal son, the happiness that is ours when we are poor in spirit comes to us as pure gift.

"Blessed are those who mourn, for they will be comforted."

The second Beatitude does not explain or spell out the mourning it names. It seems, as Bruner suggests, that the state of grief itself, of being broken-hearted, is blessed: "On Jesus' authority, in deep sadness human beings are in God's hands more than at any other time."[40] As in the first Beatitude, "Jesus puts himself on the side of outsiders, of those who aren't doing very well, of seeming failures."[41]

In his discussion of the second Beatitude, Wesley observes that the happiness that is ours when we know ourselves to be helpless before God—poor in spirit—"does not often continue long,"[42] for soon enough Jesus says, "Blessed are those who mourn." The source of their grief, according to Wesley, is not "worldly trouble or disappointment." It is not due to loss of reputation or of friends or fortune. The mourners Jesus speaks of are those who "mourn after God."[43] This is the mourning of the bitter psalmist who

39. Ibid., 56.

40. Bruner, *Matthew*, 164.

41. Ibid., 164–65.

42. Wesley, "Sermon on the Mount, Discourse I," in Wesley, *Works*, 1:483.

43. Ibid.

experiences God's hiddenness, God's silence, God's chilling absence. It is the mourning of the struggling believer whose initial joy at the "pardoning word" has given way to despair and temptation. But for those who endure it, who "tarry the Lord's leisure" (a rendering of Psalm 27 Wesley quotes from the Anglican prayerbook), they shall receive a "fresh manifestation of his love." Doubt will be swallowed up, as will all tormenting fear, and those who mourn will be comforted by the Spirit and given "full assurance of faith."[44] This "full assurance of faith," a reference to Heb 10:22, is a dominant theme in Wesley's early theology. It was something he admired in the German Moravians he encountered on his mission to the Georgia colony, and something he experienced firsthand at the famous meeting at Aldersgate in London. But later in life Wesley acknowledged "the possibility of times of darkness or doubt within restored relationship with God."[45]

But there is another kind of mourner whom Wesley speaks of: the one who weeps with those who weep (Rom 12:15). And though Wesley does not say this, here we might see Jesus as the one who makes known what blessed mourning looks like. At Bethany, Jesus weeps for his friend Lazarus and through his tears calls Lazarus forth from the grave (John 11:28–37). In that act he transforms the grief of his friends and the suspicion of his skeptics. On his way to the cross Jesus weeps over Jerusalem. Hauerwas suggests that this second Beatitude may be the most Christocentric since in Jesus's tears for the city and in his commendation of those who mourn we see that, like him, the grieving must be prepared to live in a world that does not understand true peace.[46] As Bonhoeffer puts it, "Those who mourn are those who are prepared to renounce and live without everything the world calls *happiness and peace*."[47] And then there are the tears of the woman who anoints Jesus's feet (Luke 7:36–50). Jesus blesses her mourning, even as the indignant host expresses shock and dismay.[48] Jesus is profoundly moved by the woman's actions. Perhaps he sees in her tender gestures—bathing his

---

44. Ibid., 485.

45. Maddox, *Responsible Grace*, 130.

46. Hauerwas, *Matthew*, 64.

47. Bonhoeffer, *Discipleship*, 103.

48. There are variations of this story, but it appears in all four gospels. Only in Luke does the woman weep, and only in Luke is she identified as a "sinner." In Matthew's and Mark's versions of the story Jesus says that "wherever the good news is proclaimed in the whole world, what she has done will be told in remembrance of her" (Matt 26:6–13; Mark 14:3–9). In John's Gospel it is Mary the sister of Lazarus who anoints Jesus's feet with costly nard (John 12:1–8).

feet with her tears, drying them with her hair, kissing his feet and anointing them with expensive perfume—something of the self-giving love of God that he would soon bear witness to in his own body. Through Jesus, God pours God's self out onto the world in extravagant love. This woman "wastes" her tears and her precious ointment and makes herself vulnerable to those around her in the way that divine love was made human and accessible and vulnerable in Jesus. And the gift that the anointing woman makes of her tears is received by Jesus as his heart is moved to compassion and gratitude, revealing God's own heart.

Blessed are those who weep with those who weep. In our lives we have the privilege of making a gift of our own tears as we attend to those who grieve—the wounded, the weary, the broken, the broken-hearted. But in truth we find this to be a very difficult thing. Tears are profoundly intimate. They reveal our human frailty like almost nothing else. The grieving often suffer alone because they do not know how to receive the tears of another—their own can be bewildering enough. And those who might offer comfort to the grieving by weeping with them are also often embarrassed by tears—their own and the tears of others—and at a loss for how to be so exposed and unguarded—how to simply *be with* another through suffering, unstoppable tears. But this weeping woman, blessed by Jesus, takes the risk of being vulnerable under the most extraordinary of circumstances. It is a shocking scene when we think about the social norms, prescribed gender roles, and rabbinic protocol of first-century Palestine. And we learn from her example that "God's heart calls to our hearts, inviting us to come out of ourselves, to forsake our human certainties [and] to make ourselves a gift of unbounded love."[49]

If genuine happiness is learning to be like God in goodness, then those who mourn and those who weep with them know something of the vulnerable heart of our good and gracious God.

⌇

We might imagine that the prodigal father shed many tears for his prodigal son. That in his blinding grief for his wayward child he wept like a child himself. That when he saw his son a long way off it was through a torrent of tears. And that when he ran to him and put his arms around him and kissed him there were even more tears—abundant, unstoppable tears of

---

49. Benedict XVI, Homily for the Solemnity of the Sacred Heart of Jesus.

happiness. For when one who is lost has been found, there is the deepest joy. "Blessed are those who mourn, for they will be comforted."

The Meek and Those Who Hunger and Thirst for Righteousness

"Blessed are the meek, for they will inherit the earth."

Most of us are not sure what to do with this Beatitude. In our culture meekness is often equated with weakness—we think of someone who is passive, docile, insufferably deferential. We raise our children *not* to be meek. We tend to pity the meek or to be exasperated by them. We wonder if Jesus's understanding of meekness has us missing something, but Greek scholars tell us that *praüs*, in fact, means "mild, soft, gentle." In this we are forcefully reminded, as New Testament theologian Richard Hays puts it, that "the Beatitudes limn an upside-down reality, or—more precisely—they define reality in such a way that the usual order of things is seen to be upside down in the eyes of God."[50] Blessed, indeed, to our great surprise and consternation, are the meek.

Wesley begins his treatment of this verse by stating what meekness is not. It is not ignorance or insensibility. It is not apathy or lack of zeal for God. Meekness, rather, "balances the affections"; it "keeps clear of every extreme"; it "preserves the mean in every circumstance of life." It is, at heart, "patience or contentedness." The meek do not wish to deny or extinguish any of the passions they may possess; rather, "they have mastery of all."[51]

For Wesley, what Jesus blesses in those who are meek is not only the ability to discern evil (because "they are sensible of everything of this kind"[52]) but to suffer it. We might protest: happy are those willing to *suffer*? If happiness is a matter of our becoming like God in goodness, and if God has revealed himself to us in vulnerability, in suffering love, then, in the upside-down reality of the coming reign of God, happy are those—the meek, the patient, the gentle—willing to suffer.

Here we recall two things mentioned earlier: this kind of happiness is not something we can create ourselves but something we can only receive, and it comes to us communally, not as isolated individuals. This "political" dimension of human happiness—how it is that we flourish in goodness

50. Hays, *Moral Vision of the New Testament*, 321.

51. Wesley, "Sermon on the Mount, Discourse I," in Wesley, *Works*, 1:489–90.

52. Ibid., 490.

together—helps us see that meekness is not so much an individual attribute as it is the character of a community committed to living the way of Jesus, a community seeking the goodness of God in their life together. In this we see again that the Beatitudes are not personal achievements or sentimental states or impossible ideals—they are, rather, gifts of God for the people of God for the sake of the world God loves.

We can perhaps get a better understanding of meekness as a gift to be received and practiced in community when we remember that Matthew here is alluding to Psalm 37. The promise of living in or inheriting the land is mentioned six times in this psalm as a kind of musical refrain—which, of course, it is since the Psalms were intended to be sung. And while the word *meek* is used in only one of those refrains (v. 11), other words in the other refrains give us insight into what meekness might suggest, what Matthew (and Jesus) might have meant by it:

> Trust in the LORD, and do good; so you will live in the land (v. 3)
> ... those who wait for the LORD shall inherit the land (v. 9)
> ... the meek shall inherit the land (v. 11)
> ... those blessed by the LORD shall inherit the land (v. 22)
> ... the righteous shall inherit the land (v. 29)
> ... the LORD will exalt you to inherit the land (v. 34)

The trusting and patient, the gentle and blessed, the righteous and lowly—these will inherit the land. When Jesus says, "Blessed are the meek" from the mountaintop, his Jewish hearers would have likely caught the reference. These refrains from the Psalter might even have been on their lips. When he says that the meek will inherit the earth, many in the crowd were likely thinking about land, territory, geography—about home and exile and Roman occupation. There is nothing particularly "spiritual" about this Beatitude, and Jesus's hearers are probably not thinking about it metaphorically. As Bonhoeffer notes, "Those who now possess the earth with violence and injustice will lose it, and those who renounced it here, who were meek unto the cross, will rule over the new earth."[53]

And yet we cannot say how far Matthew intends his knowing audience to take his literary allusions.[54] His is "political" speech in the sense that the Beatitudes shape a vision of a community's life together, but

---

53. Bonhoeffer, *Discipleship*, 105.

54. I am grateful to Andrew K. M. Adam for sharing with me his nuanced perspective on the use of Old Testament imagery in Matthew's Gospel.

whether he cites the Psalms for the purpose of pressing on his hearers a clear, conceptual link between Israel's exilic past and its occupied present, between the geopolitics of Judah and those of Rome, is impossible to know. Still, in Matthew's (and Jesus's) words we glimpse the revolutionary character of meekness: it is decidedly *not* weakness; it is the gentleness required to bear the folly—and the brutality—of the powerful. It is the deep patience necessary to "await God's act of putting things right."[55]

↤

For contemporary hearers and readers of this third Beatitude, the challenge is to take in what Bruner calls "one of the most breathtaking facts in Scripture: that *this* earth is to be the scene of the coming kingdom of God, this renewed earth, but *this* earth."[56] We are conditioned by Platonism, by the Enlightenment, and by some questionable theology rooted in both to believe that the coming kingdom of God will mean the fiery destruction of the earth (so why care so much for it now?) and the whisking away to heaven of the souls of the elect. But for Matthew, the promise to the meek is material and decidedly *this*-worldly: this renewed earth—the hope of which embraces both heaven and earth—will be theirs.

"Blessed are those who hunger and thirst for righteousness,
for they will be filled."

Wesley considered "righteousness" in much the same way as did the Reformation tradition generally: as the state of our being justified before God. This state is *imputed* to us (imparted, accredited, ascribed), not *accomplished* by us. This righteousness is "the mind which was in Christ Jesus," a reference to the Philippians hymn mentioned above. Jesus is the image (*eikōn*) of God; he is "in the form of God," as Philippians has it. Thus, the righteousness we hunger and thirst for is that same *imago Dei*: "the entire renewal of [the] soul in that image of God wherein it was originally created."[57]

55. Hays, *Moral Vision of the New Testament*, 98.

56. Bruner, *Matthew*, 166.

57. Wesley, "Upon Our Lord's Sermon on the Mount, II" (hereafter "Sermon on the Mount, II"), in Wesley, *Works*, 1:498.

But the word *righteousness* also connotes *holiness* for Wesley, a term he uses to mean the perfect love of God and neighbor (and a subject we will take up in greater detail in chapter 3). Such righteousness contains not only a sense of receptivity but also one of responsibility on our part. "Let me not live," Wesley prays, "but to be holy as thou art holy!"[58] When we pray such a prayer, when we hunger and thirst for this kind of holiness, we experience it as "the strongest of all our spiritual appetites. . . . It swallows up all the rest in that one great desire—to be renewed after the likeness of him that created us."[59]

Wesley is keen to warn his hearers against quenching this "blessed hunger and thirst" with what the world counts as holiness or religion: "a religion of form, of outward show, which leaves the heart as earthly and sensual as ever."[60] Abstaining from outward sin (drunkenness, say, or common swearing), being charitable to the poor, and going to church—these are the marks of a religious person in the world, says Wesley, but they alone will not satisfy one who hungers after God. True holiness is "spirit and life; the dwelling in God and God in thee."[61]

Wesley is right to take such time and care with Jesus's emphasis on *hungering* and *thirsting* for righteousness. Jesus doesn't say, "Blessed are those who *are* righteous," or "Blessed are those who practice perfect love of God and neighbor." He says, instead, blessed are those who are hungry and thirsty for such things, who painfully feel their lack. Just as Jesus quotes Isa 61:1 early in Luke's Gospel ("he has sent me to bring good news to the oppressed, to bind up the broken-hearted, to proclaim liberty to the captives, and release to the prisoners"), here in this Beatitude, like the three before it, he offers a declaration not a demand—a pronouncement of blessing rather than an ethical mandate.

And as with the Beatitude immediately before this one, it is possible that Jesus's hearers were thinking in more literal terms. In Luke's version of this Beatitude (Luke 6:21a), it clearly is about physical deprivation. Both Matthew's and Luke's audiences would have known the realities of bodily hunger and thirst all too well. Matthew's hearers especially would also have been familiar with the biblical traditions that linked God's coming reign

58. Ibid.
59. Ibid., 496.
60. Ibid., 498.
61. Ibid.

of justice and righteousness with harvests of abundance, storehouses of plenty, with joy and conviviality around shared food and drink.

> On this mountain the LORD of hosts will make for all peoples
> a feast of rich food, a feast of well-matured wines,
> of rich food filled with marrow, of well-matured wines strained clear.
> (Isa 25:6)

In our life together as the gathered people of God, the Eucharist is the shared meal of abundance in which our hunger and thirst are satisfied. In food and drink, around a table of plenty, we experience joy and conviviality as friends of one another and friends of God. Yet even in the midst of this foretaste of ultimate happiness, the Eucharist is also clear-eyed engagement with the misery and despair of *this* world; it is an act of solidarity with those whose hunger and thirst for righteousness—and whose hunger and thirst for basic bodily sustenance—have not been satisfied. Dominican priest Geoffrey Preston writes:

> Think of the domination, exploitation and pollution of man and nature that goes with bread, all the bitterness of competition and class struggle, all the organized selfishness of tariffs and price-rings, all the wicked oddity of a world distribution that brings plenty to some and malnutrition to others, bringing them to that symbol of poverty we call the bread line. And wine too—fruit of the vine and work of human hands, the wine of holidays and weddings. . . . This wine is also the bottle, the source of some of the most tragic forms of human degradation: drunkenness, broken homes, sensuality, debt. What Christ bodies himself into is bread and wine like this, and he manages to make sense of it, to humanize it. Nothing human is alien to him. If we bring bread and wine to the Lord's Table, we are implicating ourselves in being prepared to bring to God all that bread and wine mean. We are implicating ourselves in bringing to God, for him to make sense of, all which is broken and unlovely. We are implicating ourselves in the sorrow as well as the joy of the world.[62]

While learned theologians in the centuries after Jesus would develop ideas like "imputed righteousness," Matthew (and Paul) seem to assume that

---

62. Preston, *God's Way to Be Man*, 84, quoted in Radcliffe, *Why Go to Church?*, 103.

righteousness is not a "thing" God gives or grants to us; rather, Jesus himself *is* the righteousness of God that we are to become (1 Cor 1:30). When we are hungry and thirsty, Christ nourishes us with himself—with bread and wine—that we might become his body. In this, says St. Paul, is the ministry of reconciliation entrusted to us (2 Cor 5:18–21). In this, according to Matthew, our hunger and thirst are satisfied.

The Merciful, the Pure in Heart, the Peacemakers, the Persecuted

"Blessed are the merciful, for they will receive mercy."

There are a cluster of images associated with the Greek word for "mercy" in this verse. *Eleos* suggests something like "pouring out," the way oil might be dispensed from a flask.[63] Behind the Greek word is the Hebrew term *hesed*, which is also richly layered in its meanings: "loving-kindness" or "steadfast love" is one of the prime attributes of God, and so "mercy" in this sense is not pity or a wave of empathic emotion but "intentional kindness."[64]

Moreover, this is the only Beatitude in which the promise offered corresponds exactly to the condition blessed; the merciful will receive mercy. Such reciprocity is present elsewhere in Scripture, including the Lord's Prayer ("forgive us . . . as we forgive") and the letter of James ("judgment will be without mercy to anyone who has shown no mercy").

As in the previous Beatitude, we note that Jesus is declaring, not exhorting. But, as Bruner suggests, declaring *becomes* exhorting, as there is both gift and demand here: "Fullness of received mercy exists to be passed on, not stored up. Everywhere in the teaching of Jesus the test (and even sometimes, reflexively, the source) of one's relation with God is one's relation with other people (even 5:23–24 and 6:14–15 in this sermon). . . . Being a merciful, forgiving, or loving person is not a condition for God's grace, but it is a necessary consequence. Only this conclusion makes sense of this Fifth Beatitude, of the Fifth Petition of the Lord's Prayer, and of Matthew's whole Gospel."[65]

Wesley treats "merciful" in this fifth Beatitude with an extended interpretation of 1 Cor 13. For Wesley, "'the merciful,' in the full sense of

---

63. Howell, *Beatitudes for Today*, 65.

64. Mounce, *Matthew*, 40.

65. Bruner, *Matthew*, 174.

the term, are they who 'love their neighbours as themselves.'"[66] By drawing on St. Paul's famous words to illuminate this Beatitude, Wesley disabuses his readers of the notion that this kind love is sentimental or romantic or private. *Agape*—or *charity* in its deepest, richest sense—is radically, relentlessly, restlessly social; it is active in its reach, specific in its aims, articulate about what it is and what it is not. This love, says Paul, is patient, kind, forbearing, believing, hopeful, enduring. It is not envious, boastful, arrogant, or rude. It is not pushy or irritable or resentful. It does not delight in wrongdoing, but delights in the truth (1 Cor 13:4–7). And, according to Wesley, these active, specific ways of loving one's neighbor as oneself "complete the character of him that is truly merciful."[67]

Yet these qualities of character are not natural to us. Not surprisingly, self-interest ruled much of the behavior of the Corinthian Christians—the well-to-do, especially—leaving the poor and vulnerable outside the embrace of *koinonia*. Paul enjoins *agape* love on the Christians in Corinth as a condition of their being "called into the fellowship of the sacrificial meal, the *koinonia* of Christ."[68] And thus life in the *koinonia* of Christ is lived in imitation of Christ—not in accordance with our own power, intellect, cleverness, or resolve.

Author and child psychiatrist Robert Coles tells the story of his first encounter with the remarkable Dorothy Day, twentieth-century activist, journalist, and cofounder of the Catholic Worker Movement:

> It was on [an] afternoon, almost thirty-five years ago, that I first met Dorothy Day. She was seated at a table, talking with a woman who was, I quickly realized, quite drunk, yet determined to carry on a conversation. The woman . . . had a large purple-red birthmark along the right side of her forehead. She kept touching it as she uttered one exclamatory remark after another, none of which seemed to get the slightest rise from the person sitting opposite her.
>
> I found myself increasingly confused by what seemed to be an interminable, essentially absurd exchange taking place between two middle-aged women. When would it end—the alcoholic ranting and the silent nodding, occasionally interrupted by a brief question, which only served, maddeningly, to wind up the already overtalkative one rather than wind her down? Finally silence fell

66. Wesley, "Sermon on the Mount, II," in Wesley, *Works*, 1:499.

67. Ibid., 506–7.

68. Alison, *Joy of Being Wrong*, 175.

upon the room. Dorothy Day asked the woman if she would mind an interruption. She got up and came over to me. She said, "Are you waiting to talk with one of us?"[69]

Day loved her neighbor with *agape* love. The troubled, intoxicated woman was not the difficult other, the disturbed outsider, one of "them." She was not an object of pity, nor a project for moral reform. She was the neighbor whom Day had been given to love, and in showing mercy to this beloved daughter of God, Dorothy Day was one with her in the charity of Christ.

To be merciful—to love our neighbors as ourselves—is to be one in the charity of Christ. We do not conjure or summon the *feeling* of charity for the neighbor, which necessarily includes the stranger, the foreigner, and the enemy. We cannot *will* ourselves to love patiently, kindly, without envy or arrogance. Rather, in the *koinonia* of Christ—especially in the table fellowship with Christ and one another (the subject of a good deal of the first letter to the Corinthians)—we receive and learn and practice together, in fits and starts, sometimes well and sometimes poorly, the merciful ways of our merciful God.

"Blessed are the pure in heart, for they will see God."

If being merciful is not so much about our own efforts, perhaps being pure in heart is. "Purity of heart," wrote the Danish philosopher and theologian Søren Kierkegaard, is "to will one thing."[70] This one thing for Kierkegaard is *the Good*. To will, want, desire the Good is the nature of being human. As we noted earlier, Aquinas took this insight from Aristotle to make the case that happiness cannot be separated from goodness. To will this one thing, the Good, which for Kierkegaard (and Aquinas) is God, is to be pure of heart—not faultless, flawless, or sinless, but single-minded in love.[71] For the goodness of God (and, as we will see in chapter three, the truth and beauty of God) *is* God's love, God's very self.

---

69. Coles, *Dorothy Day*, 18.

70. Kierkegaard, *Purity of Heart Is to Will One Thing*, 14.

71. Kierkegaard grounds his discussion of purity of heart in Jas 4:8, which warns of "double-mindedness."

Wesley links this Beatitude to the ones preceding it and to this notion that purity of heart is single-minded love. For him, the pure in heart are those who, through the power of God's grace, have been "purified from pride by the deepest poverty of spirit; from anger, from every unkind and turbulent passion, by meekness and gentleness; from every desire but to please and enjoy God, to know and love him more and more, by that hunger and thirst after righteousness which now engrosses their whole soul: so that now they love the Lord their God with all their heart, and with all their soul, and mind, and strength."[72] As with being merciful, being pure of heart is not merely an inner state; it is also an outward way of *regarding, observing, beholding,* for the pure in heart are promised that they will see God. For Wesley, this is not a distant hope or a reward in the afterlife but an immediate reality; the pure in heart, *in the present,* "see all things full of God."[73]

Bruner notes in the Beatitudes generally and in this sixth one especially the surprising things Jesus blesses. The teachers of Jesus's day blessed devotion to Torah—faithfulness to its precepts and adherence to ritual observances. Yet in the Beatitudes, "it is difficult to put one's finger on a specific activity that is blessed, on any concrete doing, like Scripture study or like a definite kind of social work or even like times or ways of prayer."[74] Instead, Jesus seems to bless people where they are most themselves—poor in spirit, mourning, powerless, hungering for righteousness, merciful, and now pure in heart.

Similarly, Anglican priest and theologian Sam Wells sees in this sixth Beatitude a kind of habit of the heart undergirded by "uncomplicated clarity." When you are pure in heart, Wells says, you know which things are important. "Not fashionable, not popular, not effective, not lucrative, not eye-catching, not relaxing, not clever, not witty, not dramatic, not necessarily urgent: but important. And then, in a crisis, when everyone else has lost his or her sense of perspective, you'll be able to see the one thing that no one else is able to see. Because you never stopped looking at it."[75]

In the early 1960s, Canadian philosopher and former Navy officer Jean Vanier established a household in Trosly-Breuil, France, with two

---

72. Wesley, "Upon Our Lord's Sermon on the Mount, Discourse III" (hereafter "Sermon on the Mount, III"), in Wesley, *Works,* 1:510–11

73. Ibid., 513.

74. Bruner, *Matthew,* 175.

75. Wells, *Learning to Dream Again,* 139.

people with profound disabilities. This small community was the beginning of L'Arche (French for "the ark"), now "an international network of
communities in which people with intellectual disabilities live with people
who do not share that life experience."[76] For more than forty years Vanier
and the assistants in L'Arche communities have borne witness to what it
means to "live with" rather than "do for"—resisting the impulse to regard
the profoundly disabled with pity or paternalism and to see them instead
with an "uncomplicated clarity." Such purity of heart is not sentimentality.
As Vanier writes, "I get upset when people tell me, 'You're doing a good job.'
I'm not interested in doing a good job. I am interested in an ecclesial vision for community and in living in a gospel-based community with people
with disabilities. We are brothers and sisters together and Jesus is calling us
from a pyramidal society to become a body."[77]

⌖

The "uncomplicated clarity" of the pure in heart makes possible a regarding, an observing, a seeing of the God-blessed yet often world-dismissed
persons whose own uncomplicated clarity is a gift given and received. In
communities like L'Arche, there is the time and space and pace to practice
a vision of blessedness, of the happy life, that, in Wesley's words, "sees all
things full of God."[78]

"Blessed are the peacemakers, for they will be called children of God."

Wesley observes that the peace referred to in this Beatitude—*eirēnē*—is
robust and far-reaching, something like what Bruner calls "comprehensive
welfare."[79] Not merely inner tranquility or the absence of outward strife,

---

76. Hauerwas and Vanier, *Living Gently in a Violent World*, 17.

77. Ibid., 34–35. From a longtime friend of Jean Vanier, Martha Bala: "Vanier touches
others at the level of the heart, disarmed of force, with tenderness and humility. His
ability to be present to the wound within each of us is the fruit of a lifetime of fidelity to
prayer. This gift has been further honed through hours of attentive and faithful listening—to the cry of the rejected and voiceless, to the pain of others' lives, to the yearnings
of his own heart and to the tenderness of Jesus, his beloved" (http://www.jean-vanier.org/
en/the_man/presence).

78. Wesley, "Sermon on the Mount, III," in Wesley, *Works*, 1:513.

79. Bruner, *Matthew*, 177.

the peace we *make*, Wesley says, is about the good we *do*—"all manner of good."[80] A peacemaker is one who "being filled with the love of God and of all mankind cannot confine the expressions of it to his own family, or friends, or acquaintance, or party, or to those of his own opinions; no, nor those who are partakers of like precious faith; but steps over all these narrow bounds, that he may do good to every [person], that he may, some way or other, manifest his love to neighbours and strangers, friends and enemies."[81]

Here we are reminded again of something that pertains to the whole of the Sermon on the Mount, but perhaps especially to this Beatitude: Jesus's words are not directed to individuals but to the community called into being by his own life, death, and resurrection. As Hauerwas contends, "The sermon is not a heroic ethic. It is the constitution of a people. You cannot live by the demands of the sermon on your own, but that is the point."[82] In this, peacemaking is not *my* personal achievement but *our* common attempt at living into the *shalom* of God; it is "communal well-being in every direction and in every relation."[83] And, perhaps most importantly, it is formation over time—in community and friendship, through worship and acts of charity and hospitality, through struggle and uncertainty—that makes such peace possible.

And yet such peace is difficult, risky, costly. It is, paradoxically, *conflictual*. Later in Matthew's Gospel Jesus says, famously, "Do not think that I have come to bring peace to the earth. I have not come to bring peace, but a sword" (Matt 10:34). This is not the sword of violence but a sword that separates Jesus's followers from loves and loyalties that would compromise true discipleship—even the love of family. With such perplexing, provocative words, we know that Jesus must mean something very different from our usual notions of peace and peacemaking. "The way Jesus does peace," Bruner notes, "shapes the way we do it. This way is rough."[84] According to Bonhoeffer, whose own life and death bore witness to the costly, conflictual nature of peacemaking, for those who dare to follow the rough way, "their peace will never be greater than when they encounter evil people in peace

---

80. Wesley, "Sermon on the Mount, III," in Wesley, *Works*, 1:517.

81. Ibid., 518.

82. Hauerwas, *Matthew*, 61.

83. Bruner, *Matthew*, 177.

84. Ibid., 178.

and are willing to suffer from them. Peacemakers will bear the cross with their Lord, for peace was made at the cross."[85]

Peacemaking is also local and specific. For all our dreams of "world peace" (rooted, understandably, in our weariness of global wars and an earnest desire for the end of all strife and division), the peace that Jesus calls us to and that he alone makes possible is realized in mostly modest ways. It is not strategically mapped; it is not a systematic plan of action with a checklist of desired outcomes. It is, instead, a way of being that is learned and practiced over time. Christ's peace is dared, ventured, offered—quietly to an estranged friend, or publicly as a witness to powers and principalities—even when we cannot quite see the whole of it, or its end, or what it might cost us. As poet Denise Levertov puts it,

> . . . peace, like a poem,
> is not there ahead of itself,
> can't be imagined before it is made,
> can't be known except
> in the words of its making,
> grammar of justice,
> syntax of mutual aid.[86]

In the early 1940s, the remote mountain town of Le-Chambon-sur-Lignon in south central France became a place of refuge for Jews on the run from the Nazi regime. Christians—Protestant and Catholic—opened their homes to Jewish families at great risk to their own personal well-being. In a village of five thousand inhabitants, some five thousand Jews were taken in; not one who came to Le Chambon in those years was turned away. The villagers helped create false identification cards so that the Jews in their care could escape detection by the Vichy authorities; they took in orphaned children whose parents had been sent to concentration camps; they hosted celebrations of Jewish holidays. The pacifist pastor of one of Le Chambon's churches, the remarkable André Trocmé, in a sermon given the day after France signed the armistice with Germany, said, "The duty of Christians is to resist the violence that will be brought to bear on their consciences through the weapons of the spirit. We shall resist when our adversaries will

---

85. Bonhoeffer, *Discipleship*, 108.

86. Levertov, "Making Peace," in *Breathing the Water*, 40.

demand of us obedience contrary to the orders of the Gospel. We shall do so without fear, but also without pride and without hate."[87]

In his 1989 documentary film about this extraordinary community, Pierre Sauvage interviewed the surviving residents of Le Chambon, who, one after another, registered surprise in humble, graceful ways that any other response to the catastrophe of Nazism was possible.[88] For these men and women, this was the peace they were called to offer, to venture, to dare for the sake of their neighbors in distress. Not to save the world from fascism but to bear witness in their life together—in seemingly small, modest ways—to Christ who *is* our peace.

↢

Peacemakers, this Beatitude promises, will be called "children of God." Like their brother, Jesus, the children of God may discover that they are called to "step out of one entire world, where violence is always the ultimate solution, into another world, where the spiral of violence is finally broken by those willing to absorb its impact with their own flesh."[89] In times of war, in rough neighborhoods, in troubled households, this is the peace we seek to make—to venture, to dare: the costly, conflictual peace of the crucified and risen Jesus. This, as Wesley insisted, is how we manifest the love of God to neighbors and strangers, enemies and friends. This is the good we are called to do.

"Blessed are those who are persecuted for righteousness' sake,
for theirs is the kingdom of heaven."

Peacemakers are reconcilers, bringers of community, and bearers of *shalom*. But given what we have just noted about the peace Jesus calls us to, it is perhaps not surprising that in the last of the Beatitudes he prepares his followers for the unsettling truth that peacemakers will be persecuted—"put out of right relations with the community."[90] This reminds us again that the peace Christ brings will necessarily bring us into conflict. Do we really

87. Sauvage, *Weapons of the Spirit*.
88. Ibid.
89. Wink, *Powers That Be*, 97.
90. Bruner, *Matthew*, 177.

know, for example, what we are doing, what we are promising, what we are *risking* when we say so very routinely before the Eucharist "peace be with you"? The sharing of the peace has become, in many churches, little more than a momentary exchange of pleasantries. Yet it is, by contrast, both gift and command—not a conjuring of feelings of goodwill toward our nearest neighbor in the pew, but a sign of our baptismal unity as members of Christ's body. What might it mean to ponder the connection between the seventh Beatitude and the Eucharist around questions such as these: Whom do we greet when we share the peace and whom do we avoid? How does the segregated nature of many Christian churches hinder genuine reconciliation and peaceableness? How can we learn to worship with sisters and brothers with whom we have grievances that need to be addressed? How do we carry out the work of reconciliation and peacemaking in communities where even those with whom we worship are strangers to us? What do we risk when we approach the table unreconciled?[91]

In this last of the Beatitudes, Wesley recalls them all, gathering them together and noting (with some sardonic barbs) the ways in which "the world" misunderstands the states of being that Jesus calls blessed:

> They are persecuted, because they are *poor in spirit*: that is, say the world, "Poor-spirited, mean, dastardly souls, good for nothing, not fit to live in the world": because they *mourn*: "They are such dull, heavy, lumpish creatures, enough to sink anyone's spirits that sees them!" . . . because they are *meek*: "Tame, passive fools, just fit to be trampled upon"; because they *hunger and thirst after righteousness*: "A parcel of hot-brained enthusiasts, gaping after they know not what, not content with rational religion, but running mad after raptures and inward feelings"; because they are *merciful*, lovers of all, lovers of the evil and unthankful: "Encouraging all manner of wickedness" . . . because they are *pure in heart*: "Uncharitable creatures that damn all the world but those that are of their own sort!" . . . Above all because they are *peacemakers*; because they take all opportunities of doing good to all men. This is the grand reason why they have been persecuted in all ages, and will be till the restitution of all things.[92]

For Wesley, there is a "perpetual ground of enmity" between the ungodly and the children of God. And while the latter should never knowingly or "designedly" bring persecution upon themselves, it is also true, he insists,

91. See my *Teaching That Transforms*, 201–2.
92. Wesley, "Sermon on the Mount, III," in Wesley, *Works*, 1:521–22.

that persecution for righteousness' sake "is the very badge of our disciple-ship; it is one of the seals of our calling."[93] Similarly, Bonhoeffer observes that those who follow Jesus "will be offensive to the world."[94] We hardly know what to make of such words. In an era of declining church mem-bership and unquestioned, even eager, cultural accommodation (making the gospel amenable, say, to "family values" or American exceptionalism or economic prosperity), the offensiveness of Christian discipleship is not welcome news; it is not even intelligible speech. How will people be per-suaded to join our churches if we tell them that the way of Jesus will bring "not recognition, but rejection"?[95]

We know from history that bearers of such news, witnesses to it in their own bodies, are themselves often "put out of right relations with the community." It is easy to forget, for instance, how despised Martin Luther King Jr. was in his own time by many on the right and the left, by many within the church and outside it. The radical politics of the kingdom that King envisioned—for the church and the nation—did not endear him to either; it got him killed. As historian Tim Tyson bluntly puts it, "In the years since his murder, we have transformed King into a kind of innocuous black Santa Claus, genial and vacant, a benign vessel that can be filled with whatever generic good wishes the occasion dictates. . . . The radicalism of Dr. King's thought, the militancy of his methods, and the rebuke that he offered to American capitalism have given way to depictions of a man who never existed, caricatures invented after his death."[96]

Most Americans and perhaps most Christians have preferred the Martin Luther King Jr. who affirms our own outrage at racial inequality. We have not been so enthusiastic about the King who insisted that such injustice is inextricably linked to a social, political, and economic system that makes our comfortable lives possible. We have not wanted the peace of which King dreamed to cost us anything. But as the Beatitudes in Matthew's Gospel come to their conclusion, Jesus is clear that persecution is inevitable for his peacemaking followers. To make the point even more forcefully, this eighth Beatitude has a second part: "Blessed are you when people revile you and persecute you and utter all kinds of evil against you falsely on my account. Rejoice and be glad, for your reward is great in heaven, for in

93. Ibid., 525.
94. Bonhoeffer, *Discipleship*, 109.
95. Ibid.
96. Tyson, *Blood Done Sign My Name*, 107.

the same way they persecuted the prophets who were before you" (Matt 5:11–12). Another martyr of the church, Archbishop Óscar Romero of El Salvador, described it this way, ten years after the murder of King and two years before his own death by an assassin's bullet: "Even when they call us mad, when they call us subversives and communists and all the epithets they put on us, we know that we only preach the subversive witness of the Beatitudes, which has turned everything upside down to proclaim blessed the poor, blessed the thirsting for justice, blessed the suffering."[97] Romero, King, and a long line of saints and martyrs have borne witness to the madness of peaceableness in the midst of violence and all-consuming hatred. And in death, in bodies brutalized by systems propped up by fear, they summon us to our own mad, subversive, peaceable witness.

In this last Beatitude we return to the first one, where the promise is word for word the same: "theirs is the kingdom of heaven." The persecuted are given the same consolation as are the poor in spirit; they are, as Bonhoeffer says, "equal to the poor."[98] Heirs and bearers of God's reign of peace, they are also the community of the crucified, for—as we have noted all along this journey through the Beatitudes—Jesus is speaking to those who understand that the good news is also difficult news. They—we—are encouraged to "rejoice and be glad." And "from that eternal joy there comes a call to the community of disciples here under the cross, the call of Jesus, 'blessed, blessed.'"[99]

Summary

"You are made to be happy in God." John Wesley wrote these words in a sermon on the unity of the triune God.[100] As we come to the end of the Beatitudes and his extensive treatment of them, we have seen the strange and beautiful call of discipleship that locates happiness in poverty of spirit, mourning, meekness, the hunger and thirst for righteousness, mercy,

---

97. Romero, *Violence of Love*, 48.
98. Bonhoeffer, *Discipleship*, 109.
99. Ibid., 110.
100. Wesley, "The Unity of Divine Being."

purity of heart, peacemaking, and persecution for righteousness' sake. We are mindful that this is not the happiness that advertisers wish to sell us. In conversation with voices from the church catholic, we have noted that the Wesleyan tradition holds that to be happy is to become like God in goodness—to flourish together in community just as the Father, Son, and Holy Spirit dwell in mutual love and generosity. What Jesus calls "blessed," what counts as happiness in the Christian life, is not separate from him. In him is the goodness of God made known. In him do we come to know what it means to be happy, what it means to be human.

Questions for Consideration

1. Currently, in Western culture, what counts as a "happy life"? Provide examples.

   a. What does it mean that consumerism trains us or teaches us to be dissatisfied?

   b. How does such dissatisfaction relate to the desire to acquire more things?

2. How has the Christian tradition defined ultimate happiness?

   a. What does "becoming like God in goodness" (Aquinas) look like, and how does such goodness relate to happiness?

   b. How does the insight that "the God who wants our good gifts us with the happiness we seek" (Wadell) contrast with wider cultural assumptions regarding happiness discussed earlier?

   c. How is happiness "ineluctably political," that is, social and communal, and related to such practices as baptism and Eucharist? How does this view of happiness conflict with individualistic interpretations of happiness?

3. What does Jesus's life reveal about the nature of happiness and the relation of happiness to blessedness?

   a. How does Jesus's preaching of the Beatitudes reveal them to be a way of life in community rather than a "prescription for self-actualization" or a set of "impossible ideals"?

   b. How does the school of thought known as "Christian realism" (Niebuhr) miss the deeper reality of the church itself as social body summoning us to a whole new way of life of happiness together?

   c. How does John Wesley's threefold pattern of understanding the Sermon on the Mount speak of those "states of blessedness" that can produce lives of happiness and holiness, that is, lives that avoid those "emotions contrary to God"? How does this view differ from Christian realism? How might the Wesleyan view be considered *more* "realistic"? Explain.

4. What does Jesus mean when he commends that state of blessedness known as "poor in spirit"?

   a. What is the connection between happiness and "poor in spirit," between happiness and coming home?

   b. How does Wesley's view of "poor in spirit" as total dependence on God lead to a picture of happiness? Is Wesley's understanding of sin as both offense and illness helpful in diagnosing where humans fall short? How does Wesley's view offer a critique of Western cultural assumptions about happiness?

5. What does it mean to say that "those who mourn shall be comforted"?

   a. What are the two ways Wesley understands mourning?

   b. How are these two ways of understanding mourning related to genuine happiness? What kind of tears may we need to shed as part of this state of blessedness?

6. What does the Beatitude of meekness mean in relation to the inheritance of the earth?

   a. What is meekness? What is it not?

   b. What does John Wesley see in this Beatitude with respect to happiness?

   c. What, in Wesley's understanding of this Beatitude, may prompt a negative reaction as it pertains to modern notions of self-importance or autonomy?

   d. What are the possible misconceptions this Beatitude may have on contemporary readers, especially with respect to political power and earthly stewardship?

7. What does it mean that those who hunger and thirst for righteousness will be filled?

   a. How does the Wesleyan assessment of hungering and thirsting for holiness and righteousness reveal the strongest of our spiritual appetites, or that desire to be renewed in likeness of God? How does such a desire conflict with those desires trained otherwise in the market economy?

   b. What is the importance of the Eucharist in satisfying the hunger and thirst for righteousness? What role does the Eucharist have in cultivating those desires that can lead to abundant life, to happiness, to becoming Christ's own body in and for the world?

8. What does the Beatitude "blessed are the merciful, for they will receive mercy" mean?

   a. What does the word *mercy* mean? Share.

   b. How is Wesley's employment of the word *love* or *agape* revealing of the active character of mercy in the fullest sense, that is, as revealing of who Christ is in the community, as loving one's neighbor as oneself?

   c. Share ways in which practicing such mercy can lead to happiness.

9. How will the "pure in heart see God"?

   a. What does purity of heart mean to Wesley? How does it relate to his understanding of God's grace?

   b. How do other thinkers help clarify what this Beatitude entails (e.g., Aquinas, Kierkegaard, Wells, Vanier)?

10. What does the Beatitude "blessed are the peacemakers, for they will be called children of God" mean?

   a. What is the nature of the peace Jesus commends in this Beatitude?

   b. How do notions of "heroic individualism" silence the communal nature of this peace? What is lost in such a distortion?

   c. How is the witness of the mountain town of Le Chambon-sur-Lignon in France during World War II an example of the kind of peacemaking being encouraged here? Are such examples "realistic"?

   d. What does it mean to be children of God in light of the practice of peacemaking?

11. What does the Beatitude "blessed are those who are persecuted for righteousness' sake" entail?

   a. What is the connection between the sharing of such peace and persecution? How do the peace and righteousness that Christ brings lead us into conflict? Explain.

   b. Do we really understand what we are saying when, before the Eucharist, we say, "Peace be with you"? Offer personal experiences.

    c. How is being persecuted for righteousness' sake the very badge of discipleship? Do persons who attend our churches view this as such? What are the ways we accommodate or "water down" this state of blessedness (happiness) because of the surrounding culture, thus losing the offense of the gospel? What other examples, in addition to King and Romero, might we want to list? Share.

12. Based on the above commentary, how is the call to discipleship truly also the call to happiness, the call to become like God in goodness?

two

Health: The Christian Life and the Shalom of God

I was, as the prophet said, hungering and thirsting for righteousness. I found it at the eternal and material core of Christianity: body, blood, bread, wine, poured out freely, shared by all.

—Sara Miles, *Take This Bread*

Author of life divine,
Who hast a table spread,
Furnished with mystic wine
And everlasting bread.

—Charles Wesley, Hymn 40, in *Hymns on the Last Supper*

Food is the daily sacrament of unnecessary goodness, ordained for a continual remembrance that the world will always be more delicious than it is useful.

—Robert Farrar Capon, *The Supper of the Lamb*

Being Happy, Being Healthy

Scientists now have compelling data for what most people have always in-tuited as true: the happier we are the healthier we are.[1] We live in a time of unprecedented concern for our physical well-being. "Fitness" is a mul-tibillion-dollar-a-year industry, something our forebears even fifty years ago would be at a loss to understand. How would I explain to my robust, outdoorsy grandparents that I sometimes pay money to go into a large win-dowless room to exercise among strangers, each of us running in place on our own complex machine while listening to music that no one else can hear? Yet along with this obsession with fitness and physical well-being, our culture faces a number of alarming health crises, many of them affecting the young. Part of this paradox is explained by economics: the affluent have the time and money to attend to their health (gym memberships and access to good medical care) in ways that the poor do not.

But what does this have to do with "the Christian life"? We do not often think of bodily health in theological terms. We have been taught in ways both subtle and overt that what matters for the Christian life is our *spiritual* well-being. From Greek philosophy—not from Scripture, as we will see—we have inherited a dualistic view of the human person: the no-tion that each of us is an immortal soul housed in a temporary body. This bifurcation of the physical and the spiritual is so entrenched in our think-ing that we can hardly imagine our way out of it. But such a division does not describe the way things are so much as it *invents* a way of understand-ing and naming the human person. From the beginning, followers of Jesus have been attracted to various forms of this stark, dualistic view of human nature and its inherent privileging of soul over body, spirit over matter, heaven over earth—its *de*valuing, in fact, of the whole material creation. Some of the early Christian texts associated with this view insisted that Jesus only *seemed* to be human, only *seemed* to suffer and die on the cross.

But Scripture gives witness to a deeply incarnational faith. The God of the Bible is embarrassingly particular. Yahweh calls a people and dwells in the midst of them. In John's Gospel we read that the *Logos* became a human being and "tabernacled" among us (John 1:14). This Word who became

---

1. Boehm and Kubzansky, "The Heart's Content." Earlier research in this area has focused primarily on how risk factors like anxiety and depression are associated with heart disease. This investigation is considered the first to establish that "health assets" (such as optimism) are also associated with heart health. See also http://www.rwjf.org/en/blogs/pioneering-ideas/2012/04/happiness-is-hot-1.html.

flesh was present "in the beginning" when the cosmos was formed, when all of creation was pronounced *good*. The material world, in the world of Scripture, matters deeply. Bodies matter. The Word made flesh, Jesus of Nazareth, was born into the material realities of poverty and vulnerability, of scandal, gossip, and political oppression. "Nothing human," Geoffrey Preston observes, "is alien to him."[2]

And as we noted in chapter 1, the happiness we long for, seek, and receive as gift—our becoming more like God in goodness—is available to us only in material ways, in *embodied* practices and habits of being cultivated over time. We are merciful or peaceable, we mourn and we are meek, insofar as we do certain things in and with our bodies and to, for, and with other bodies.

Even the ultimate happiness we hope for—eternal communion with the God who made the world and called it good—is not described in Scripture as a state of being that comes to us after our souls escape our bodies, after we have flown away into heaven "leaving this world behind," as many old gospel hymns would have it. Rather, as Anglican theologian N. T. Wright has argued, salvation and its ultimate realization is about whole human beings, not disembodied souls. It is about the present and not simply the future. And it has to do with what God does *through* us, not only what God does in and for us.[3] When we consider salvation, health, happiness, and the hope of heaven all of a piece in this way, we understand that "what you do with your body in the present matters because God has a great future in store for it. . . . What you do in the present—by painting, preaching, singing, sewing, praying, teaching, building hospitals, digging wells, campaigning for justice, writing poems, caring for the needy, loving your neighbor as yourself—will last into God's future. These activities are not simply ways of making the present life a little less beastly, a little more bearable. . . . They are part of what we may call building for God's kingdom."[4]

As this chapter seeks to show, salvation as a theological category and as lived reality has to do with health in the most literal of ways. The grace that rescues, redeems, restores, and reconciles comes to us as the whole selves we are—body, mind, spirit—not merely to our intellects as knowledge to which we give assent or approval. In the New Testament, the Greek

2. Preston, *God's Way to Be Man*, 84.

3. Wright, *Surprised by Hope*, 201.

4. Ibid., 193.

word for "salvation," *sōzō*, implies cure, remedy, recovery.[5] The hope is that what is broken will be made whole, what is infirm or afflicted, what has languished or suffered or despaired—all will be brought to fullness of life, to health and well-being in the communion of divine love, in the peace and goodness of God. This, we learn repeatedly from Genesis to Revelation, is God's deepest desire for all that God has made.

Earlier we noted that when Jesus announces the kingdom of God he is speaking of and bearing witness in his own being to God's reign of love, mercy, and generosity. This rule or reign is glimpsed when and where fullness of life, health, and well-being are experienced. Another word from Scripture that captures the wide expanse of all these ways of naming what the salvation of God looks like is *shalom*. In chapter 1 we noted that the peacemakers of the seventh Beatitude are those who not only address conflict but who venture to practice this fullness of life that signals the health and wholeness God desires for all.

Salvation, *shalom*, like all things from God, is a gift, and the gift of salvation, the gift of Jesus Christ himself, comes to us in and through the material order. Salvation comes in divine love made incarnate in a human family in first-century Palestine. It comes in the life and ministry of this one who went about teaching and preaching, feeding hungry bodies and healing broken and diseased bodies. It comes to us in Word and Sacrament—in our encounter with Scripture and in the bread and wine of the Eucharist that nourishes and heals.

The Eucharist, the church's holy meal, partaking of which was considered by Wesley to be a Christian's "constant duty," is not mere symbolic act or ceremonial escapism from the mundane realities of life.[6] It is not a minimizing or avoidance of the daily struggles we experience in our bodies—loneliness or grief, illness or infirmity, injustice or oppression. Rather, these difficult realities are taken up into this shared meal of true companionship. A companion is one with whom one shares bread (*com* = with; *panis* = bread). In the Eucharist we eat with each other and in so doing are made friends with God. The Eucharist is where our hungry bodies become the one body of Christ, that we might be companions to hungry neighbors. "There are so many hungry people among us," a Brazilian priest once observed, "that God would only dare to appear in the form of bread."[7]

5. Coogan, "Salvation," 670.

6. Wesley, "The Duty of Constant Communion."

7. Quoted in Scheper-Hughes, *Death without Weeping*, 519.

Eating together at the Lord's Table—this central act of the church's common life—ought to inform all our thinking and acting about wholeness and well-being, about the fullness of life, *shalom*, that is God's desire for all that God has made. The health of our bodies, of our communities, of creation itself is, at heart, a eucharistic concern.

Wesley on Health

John Wesley cared a great deal about physical well-being. We might even say that he, like many a gym-going fitness fanatic today, was a little obsessed. He collected thousands of remedies and cures for everything from asthma, earache, ringworm, and rickets to sciatica, scurvy, shingles, and ulcers—many recommended from personal experience ("Tried. Seldom fails," he would write in his journal). In the eighth year of the existence of British Methodism, 1747, Wesley published *Primitive Physick: Or, an Easy and Natural Method of Curing Most Diseases.*[8] There were twenty-four editions of the book by 1792.

This venture in giving medical advice by an Anglican clergyman is not as strange as it may seem to us. Medical tracts were popular in eighteenth-century England, and they were written especially for those who lacked access to a health care "system" that existed primarily for the aristocracy and the wealthy. The Royal College of Physicians in London, for instance, began as "an exclusive domain of upper-class medical practitioners . . . a professional guild of the elect . . . for persons with similar interests and a joint determination to enhance the standing of their profession."[9] For the poor, medical tracts and pamphlets were often their first and last source for instructions on how to treat a range of maladies. And the authors of such documents were commonly not physicians, a fact, writes historian Samuel Rogal, "that had little or no bearing upon the quality of the advice set forth on the printed page. Since, during the seventeenth and eighteenth centuries, medical knowledge was neither voluminous nor complicated, the majority of educated individuals believed that they could dispense 'practical physick' with as much confidence, if not actual competence, as a surgeon, physician, or apothecary."[10]

8. Wesley, *Primitive Physick*. All references here are to this edition.

9. Stevens, *Medical Practice in Modern England*, 12, quoted in Rogal, "Pills for the Pill," 81.

10. Rogal, "Pills for the Pill," 82.

Wesley's advice on matters of physical health has been widely ridiculed and dismissed—in his own time and in the generations since. His prescriptions can amuse: "To cure baldness: Rub the part morning and evening, with onions, till it is red; and rub it afterwards with honey. Or wash it with a decoction of boxwood: Tried. Or, electrify it daily."[11] Wesley was fascinated with the burgeoning field of electric shock therapy and convinced of its effectiveness for treating a host of infirmities. He regularly practiced it on himself with his own personal machine. (Not so amusing, perhaps). And some of his ideas were surely reckless, even dangerous: recommending, for example, quicksilver (mercury) for a variety of ailments—a "remedy" prescribed routinely in the eighteenth century.

But Wesley's *interest* in the subject (and his passion for it) have some interesting roots. He was harshly critical of the medical establishment's elitism—its disregard for the lower classes—and its rejection of natural remedies in favor of an "abundance of compound medicines, consisting of so many ingredients, that it was scarce possible for common people to know which it was that wrought the cure—abundance of exotics, neither the nature nor names of which their own countrymen understood."[12] There is something of a parallel here with Wesley's disdain for the clerical elitism of his day—with what he perceived to be the Church of England's lack of pastoral care and material concern for the poor. Just as Wesley felt compelled to take the gospel to coal miners and factory workers and the urban underclass through his practice of open air preaching, he was also moved to address the needs of these same vulnerable women, men, and children, as they had little recourse for dealing with the inevitable illnesses and injuries of life—the non-life-threatening as well as the catastrophic.

There is also a compelling simplicity to Wesley's overall view of human health and to the advice he dispenses (his many odd and questionable cures notwithstanding)—a simplicity that resonates with much recovered wisdom on the subject in our own time. When, for example, in the preface to *Primitive Physick*, Wesley advises his readers to eat simple foods in moderate portions, and always more vegetables than meat, one almost hears contemporary food writer Michael Pollan's simple rule: "Eat food. Not too much. Mostly plants."[13] And who can complain about these sound instructions from Wesley: "Use as much exercise daily in the open air, as you can

11. Wesley, *Primitive Physick*, 35–36.

12. Ibid., vii.

13. Pollan, *Food Rules*, 17.

without weariness. Sup at six or seven on the lightest food; go to bed early, and rise betimes. To persevere with steadiness in this course, is often more than half the cure."[14]

The Wesleys on the Eucharist

It may seem strange that the early Methodist movement—with its open-air preaching and itinerant clergy, its mission to the North American frontier, its reputation for revivalistic fervor and heartfelt piety—would place such a premium on the sacrament of Holy Communion. An emphasis on the Eucharist and insistence on its frequent celebration is generally considered to be associated with high-church formality, with elaborate, ceremonial liturgies. But for brothers John and Charles Wesley, the celebration of the Eucharist was central to the Christian life. Partaking of the sacrament was such an integral part of the Wesley brothers' life as college students at Oxford that their predictable, dependable, *methodical* pattern of receiving the Lord's Supper daily earned them the epithet "Methodists" from their bemused peers. And as John wrote later in one of his sermons, "Let everyone therefore who has either any desire to please God, or any love of his own soul, obey God and consult the good of his own soul by communicating every time he can; like the first Christians with whom the Christian sacrifice was a *constant part of the Lord's day's service*."[15]

What is also striking in the theology and hymnody of the Wesleys is that they viewed the Eucharist in an *eschatological* light—as a "foretaste of the heavenly banquet," a sharing in the not-yet-fully-realized abundance and well-being that God intends for all of creation. Earlier theological discussions of the Eucharist—both Protestant and Catholic—tended to focus on the question of real presence in the sacrament and on the meaning of the eucharistic sacrifice. The hotly contested debates of the sixteenth-century, especially, bear witness to the intensity of the polemics devoted to these doctrinal matters. The Wesleys do indeed treat such questions and concerns, but unlike the earlier reformers, there is in their sermons and songs a clear emphasis on the meal's eschatological dimension—most evident in their collection *Hymns on the Lord's Supper*, published in 1745.

---

14. Wesley, *Primitive Physick*, vii.

15. Wesley, "The Duty of Constant Communion." Wesley's italics.

> To heaven the mystic banquet leads;
> Let us to heaven ascend,
> And bear this joy upon our heads
> Till it in glory end.[16]

The church's celebration of the Lord's Supper anticipates and glimpses the abundance of the heavenly feast in the fullness of God's *shalom*; it is, in the words of the Wesleys, the "pledge of heaven." It is, as Wesleyan scholar Colin Williams has noted, "a pledge of the climactic banquet with Christ which there awaits us."[17] And when we consider the feasting scenes in the gospels—when and where and how Jesus eats with his disciples, his friends, his followers, his enemies—we see that the invitation is always open to all, and that these celebrations with food and drink are also always occasions for hospitality to strangers and outcasts, for healing and reconciliation, for surprising glimpses of the *shalom* of God.[18]

This eschatological emphasis in the Wesleys' eucharistic theology is also profoundly *communal*. As we saw in the first chapter, classic Christian doctrine holds that our life in God is our life *together* in God. The happiness we were made for is relentlessly social; the *shalom* of God is deeply *political*. That is, we flourish and thrive, we experience health and wholeness in relationship with others and as sharers in the indwelling love of the triune God. Another eucharistic hymn captures the sense that the eschatological promise—ultimate happiness in God, "the life of heaven"—is lived, however imperfectly, in the present:

> Saviour of life, and joy, and bliss,
> Pardon and power and perfect peace
> We shall herewith receive:
> The grace implied through faith is given,
> And we that eat the Bread of heaven
> The life of heaven shall live.[19]

This understanding of the church as a social body is pervasive in John Wesley's writing and is particularly evident in his penchant for method and accountability. For him, the Christian life is not a private enterprise or an

16. Hymn 99, in Rattenbury, *Eucharistic Hymns of John and Charles Wesley*, 225.

17. Williams, *John Wesley's Theology Today*, 165.

18. See for instance Luke 14:7–24.

19. Hymn 56, in Rattenbury, *Eucharistic Hymns of John and Charles Wesley*, 212.

individual quest but a shared, communal way of living and bearing witness in the world. It is a life that can be lived well only within the context of mutual discipleship, a context that makes possible the upbuilding of believers in their lifelong journey together as followers of the way of Jesus.

This social aspect of the Christian life is nowhere more evident than in Wesley's fourth discourse on the Sermon on the Mount: "I shall endeavour to show," he writes, "that Christianity is essentially a social religion, and that to turn it into a solitary religion is indeed to destroy it."[20] And he continues, "When I say this is essentially a social religion, I mean not only that it cannot subsist so well, but that it cannot subsist at all without society, without living and conversing with other men."[21]

Wesley's creation of the class meeting—a weekly gathering of persons who agreed to exercise mutual accountability for their Christian discipleship—was the result of his insistence that the Christian life is not a one-on-one proposition between a person and God but rather a relationship with the triune God that could be mediated only by the community gathered in worship, friendship, and truth-telling. The Methodist "societies," of which the class meetings were subgroups, were for Wesley integral to the edification of the whole church. The promise made by each of the members was "to speak, each of us in order, freely and plainly the true state of our souls, with the faults we have committed in thought, word, or deed, and the temptations we have felt since our last meeting."[22] It is worth noting that the class meetings emerged out of the kitchen gatherings of Susannah Wesley, the devout and influential mother of John and Charles, reminding us that the Wesleyan vision of communal discipleship had its origins in the practical, everyday activities of maintaining a household. The baking of bread in these kitchens is also a compelling image in relation to the bread of the Eucharist.

Within this context of accountable discipleship, of recognizing that the Eucharist makes of us a *social* body, Wesley insists on not only frequent but "constant" communion. At a time when the Anglican Church was experiencing a general decline in celebrations of the Eucharist (only three a year were required in most parish churches), Wesley warned, "Whoever therefore does not receive . . . either does not understand his duty or does not

20. Wesley, "Sermon on the Mount, Discourse III," in Wesley, *Works*, 1:533.

21. Ibid., 534.

22. Wesley, "Rules of the Band Societies," 77.

care for the dying command of his Saviour, the forgiveness of his sins, the strengthening of his soul, and the refreshing of it with the hope of glory."[23]

If John Wesley was a man of his own time in regard to the medical advice he dispensed, he and his hymn-writer brother, Charles, were also typical eighteenth-century churchmen in that they did not make a direct link between the Eucharist and bodily health and well-being. Wesley is insistent that the primary reason the faithful receive the body and blood of Christ is that Jesus commanded it, and in so doing we receive the mercy of God: forgiveness of sins and strength for living. These are spiritual gifts in Wesley's thinking. "As our bodies are strengthened by bread and wine," he writes, "so are our souls by these tokens of the body and blood of Christ. This is the food of our souls."[24] In the Twenty-five Articles of Religion, Wesley's adaptation of the Anglican Church's Thirty-nine Articles, he says that Christians consume the body of Christ "only after a heavenly and spiritual manner."[25]

But these claims are less about promoting the kind of dualistic anthropology discussed earlier and more about Wesley giving voice to his anti-Roman sentiments. His continual concern when discussing the sacrament is to avoid aligning his views—and thus the views of the nascent Methodist movement—with the doctrine of transubstantiation. But even here it is more complicated than that. While Wesley writes disparagingly of Catholic doctrine (as did most of his Protestant contemporaries), the eucharistic theology in his sermons and especially in his and Charles's hymns displays what liturgical scholar Don Saliers calls "a profound convergence between Catholic and Evangelical theology in relation to the Eucharist."[26] Saliers notes that the communion hymns make use of several themes that would have been considered suspect by the Wesleys' fellow reformers: a devotion to the wounds of Christ, the language of blood atonement, and images related to sacrifice.[27]

23. Wesley, "The Duty of Constant Communion."

24. Ibid.

25. Article 18, cited in Oden, *Doctrinal Standards in the Wesleyan Tradition*, 121.

26. Saliers, "Introduction," in Rattenbury, *Eucharistic Hymns of John and Charles Wesley*, vi.

27. Ibid. Here is one example, the first stanza of a hymn written by John and published in the 1740 edition of *Hymns and Sacred Poems*:

I thirst, Thou wounded Lamb of God,
To wash me in thy cleansing blood,
To dwell within thy wounds; then pain
Is sweet, and life or death is gain.

For our purposes, we can acknowledge these contextual realities and the limits of Wesley's vision as it relates to eucharistic practice and bodily health. But we can also appreciate how his deep compassion for those who suffer in body, mind, and spirit fits with his eschatological interpretation of the sacrament: that the bread and wine we share as friends of God and one another anticipates the *shalom* of heaven, even as it calls us to a renewed understanding of salvation as well-being for all in the here and now.

The Unhealthy Body of Christ

At the heart of this modest meal is simple food: a bit of bread and a sip of wine or juice. Despite its simplicity, or perhaps because of it, Christians have argued about this supper for centuries. What does it mean? Who can serve it? Who may eat it, and when? In recent years other concerns have been added to these—concerns regarding the Eucharist's relationship to other meals, to the daily bread we consume for physical strength and sustenance—and thus new questions have arisen. Where does our daily food come from? What are its costs—not only to ourselves but to land, resources, animals, and workers? Why do millions of people lack access to good food while the rest of us waste so much of it?

These questions are deeply political in both senses of the word: they are rooted in the partisan politics that drive public policy around issues of food production and distribution, and they have to do with how a society orders its common life for the flourishing of all—or how it fails to do so. In the Eucharist we feast at creation's table, finding ourselves linked to all the world and especially to those creatures—human and nonhuman—who suffer and are exploited for our gain. So, for instance, the cheap turkeys we are able to buy for our holiday feasts actually come at a considerable cost that someone must pay, namely, the low-wage workers who process thousands of birds a day in dirty, dangerous conditions. If these workers are undocumented, they likely do not feel free or safe enough to complain. And the birds themselves—the big-breasted poultry we have come to expect, if not demand—are raised to be that way; they are overfed corn (not their natural sustenance) to dramatically (and painfully) accelerate the growing process. They are kept in cramped, dark "houses" where, under the stress of their own grotesque body weight, their small legs collapse and they spend their brief lives lying and squirming in their own excrement. We may joke that we can't get up from the table after gorging on turkey and all the trimmings;

what we may not know is the animals we are eating likely couldn't move much either.

These "political" matters are profoundly theological and eucharistic. Theologian Norman Wirzba argues compellingly that all of creation, human and nonhuman, participates in the salvation and reconciliation that God desires for all that God has made:

> We can spend a lot of time debating whether or not Paul and the early Christians really believed worms, plants, and bees to be included in God's salvation of the world. In certain respects, the debate is beside the point. Unless we believe that God cares only about disembodied souls—a position consistently condemned by the church as heretical—then it is all of creation or none of it that God will save. Human life simply makes no sense apart from the life of all creation. We live only because the worms, plants and bees do too. And they live because God loves them.[28]

In light of this truth, the Eucharist is always justice in the midst of injustice, reconciliation in the midst of enmity and estrangement, sharing in the midst of accumulation and hoarding, communal conviviality in the midst of private pain and loneliness. To be grateful for the gifts that sustain and enrich our lives is to take responsibility for our own habits that unwittingly deny the intrinsic goodness of the earth and everything—*everything*—that dwells in it.

It is not only the Lord's Supper but all of Scripture that raises these concerns and others like them. Throughout the Bible we encounter a God who links food with justice: who hears the cries of the hungry and blesses with harvests of abundance; who chastises the gluttonous and the overfed; who reconciles the estranged through simple meals or fatted-calf feasts. In the gospels, it is Jesus's table fellowship with social outcasts that most confounds his critics. He tells stories about seeds and soil, farmers and bakers. When he feeds the hillside multitudes with bread and fish, all four evangelists are keen to tell us that full bellies and plenty of leftovers for others are signs of the reign of God. And in Jesus's last meal before his execution, he reworks Israel's signature ritual feast to offer his own body and blood as food for his closest companions.[29]

28. Wirzba, "Reconciliation with the Land," in Bahnson and Wirzba, *Making Peace with the Land*, 24.

29. As Matthew Whelan observes, "when he takes the bread, breaks it, shares it, tells his disciples that the bread is his body and that they should 'do this in remembrance' of him, he speaks of a way of living in which his followers' bodies, like his, are to be gifts for

Now we who have been baptized into his death live by consuming Christ. His body—taken, blessed, broken, and shared—makes of us a body. And for all that this means and for all that it requires, there is this fundamental imperative: we are to nourish and care for our own bodies and the bodies of others. Thus all our sharing of food (and our withholding or wasting of it), our complicity with unjust food systems, and, perhaps most unsettling, all our eating (and overeating) are implicated in our participation in this simple meal.

So what are we to make of the unhealthy, overweight body we have become? How do we address—with grace, not judgment—the alarming rise in food-related illness and obesity in the bodies of men, women, and children who are members of the eucharistic body?

According to the Centers for Disease Control, since 1980 obesity prevalence in children and adolescents has more than tripled. One-third of all adults in the United States are obese, and more than 60 percent are overweight. And for the foreseeable future these numbers are only expected to increase. Rates for type-2 diabetes have skyrocketed, especially among the young—something no one could have predicted even fifty years ago. New cases of coronary heart disease, stroke, and cancer continue to exceed all predictions. Our unhealthy lifestyle choices—mostly having to do with food—contribute significantly to the staggering rise in health care costs.

As grim as these facts are, they are almost never interpreted theologically or pastorally. The radical individualism of modern Western Christianity and the body-spirit dualism mentioned earlier train us to consider eating and our choices and habits regarding food as both intensely personal and unrelated to "faith." When, for example, Christians have sought to heed St. Paul's admonition to "present your bodies as living sacrifices" (Rom 12:1) we have not thought so much about food as about vice, interpreting the passage as a summons to abstinence—abstinence from sex for the unmarried and from the evils of drinking and smoking (and sometimes dancing and gambling) for all.

But there is also the outright awkwardness of talking about overeating and obesity in almost any context. Our culture trains us from the time we are very young to be conscious of body types and to make moral judgments about certain shapes and sizes. It is not news to point out that for a hundred years fashion magazines have fetishized an impossibly thin, ideal female

the nourishment of others. Such bodies are eucharistic: the spirit that moves them is one of concern for the nourishment of others." Whelan, "The Responsible Body."

form. In recent decades, publications like *GQ* and *Esquire* have done the same for male readers. Even when such objectification of the human form is resisted, even when we recognize it as a strategy of consumer capitalism, most of us—women *and* men—carry lifelong anxiety about our bodies, especially about the appearance of our bodies. And how much we weigh is often the centerpiece of our worry.

There are a number of other reasons why conversations about eating and overeating are difficult to have in ecclesial settings. First, there is the role that fellowship meals have long played in congregational life: potluck suppers, dinner on the ground—any number of occasions at which Christians gather around tables of plenty. Perhaps especially in the South these meals have featured the richest of foods, labor-intensive and time-consuming in their preparation: the fried chicken feast with its many accompanying dishes, tables heavy laden with decadent cakes and pies. Overeating at these communal meals seems almost an obligation—all that effort!—a way to compliment and honor the cooks. To bring up the sin of gluttony in such a context seems a lapse in good table manners.

Church suppers are also linked powerfully to memory and to long-term Christian formation. Through the years parishioners might not remember what Epiphany is or how many Sundays are in Ordinary Time, but they recall with fondness a favorite dish lovingly prepared and brought every year to the church picnic. They also sense, rightly, the power of food to create and strengthen community. Shared meals over time are significant occasions for both practicing and growing in faithful Christian witness— for learning to offer and receive hospitality, for cultivating attentiveness to the goodness of creation, for being leisurely present to others in this era of eating fast and eating alone. In ordinary table fellowship (as in the Eucharist) we meet each other at the level of our most basic need. As Frederick Buechner has observed, "It is hard to preserve your dignity with butter on your chin or to keep your distance when asking for the tomato ketchup."[30] When we eat together we make ourselves available and vulnerable to one another and thus glimpse and share in something of the mystery and beauty of divine communion. Now someone wants to spoil these powerful experiences with depressing health statistics?

Second, a dramatic rise in the number of overweight clergy makes preaching, teaching, and pastoral counseling about obesity awkward and difficult. In recent years studies have shown what many clergy, their

30. Buechner, *Wishful Thinking*, 65.

spouses, and attentive laypeople have long known: that pastors often suffer in silence and isolation the stresses and burdens of congregational ministry. Loneliness, depression, addiction, the breakup of marriages—these and other painful realities of life in the fishbowl of ordained ministry take a tremendous toll on the physical and emotional well-being of clergypersons and their families. In North Carolina, for example, a state that ranks as the twelfth worst in the nation in terms of the percentage of obese citizens, the Clergy Health Initiative at Duke Divinity School has discovered that rates of chronic disease and obesity in the state's pastors are significantly higher than those of their non-clergy peers. And yet until recently little has been said, let alone done, to even acknowledge the problem. Thankfully, efforts like those of the Clergy Health Initiative have begun to break the silence, provide resources, and effect positive changes for pastors, families, and congregations. But as welcome as these developments are, there persists a general lack of pastoral leadership on the inherent connections between food (and food-related health concerns) and Christian discipleship.

Third, sociological factors make it difficult to talk about obesity in the church and to frame the issue of overeating eucharistically. Women and girls who struggle with body image issues, for instance, who are trying to resist or have finally conquered the cultural pressures to be unrealistically thin, must now negotiate health warnings about the serious risks of being too fat. And what is "too fat" from the perspective of optimum health? And how (and why) have congregations failed to be hospitable places for those suffering from both the silent shame and poor physical health that accompany any number of eating disorders? And eating and body image concerns are not exclusive to women and girls; matters related to food and self-worth go deep for both genders.

Class issues also come into play. Is the current trend toward questioning our food sources and eating more responsibly the privilege of those with the time and resources to pursue such ethics? What are the social and economic conditions that keep many of the working poor in perpetual poor health? And how is it possible for congregations to address these questions honestly and fruitfully when so many churches are segregated by class?

And in terms of race, food and identity go deep. Whether it's the soul food tradition of African-American cuisine, the carb/corn-rich diet of Latino cultures, or the "never enough" butter and salt of white Southern cooking, food and shared mealtime rituals profoundly shape racial and cultural identity—and routinely lead to increased risk for heart disease, diabetes, and obesity. Yet what would those Sunday potlucks be without the beloved dishes—homey, comfort fare—of one's ethnic heritage? Still, since most churches are segregated largely by race, and since racial identity markers are often assumed to trump baptism and Eucharist as that which make of Christians one body, too many congregations are short on the theological resources to locate alternatives to poor eating habits not just in desired health outcomes but in the food and fellowship shared by the baptized at the Table of the Lord.

A fourth and final reason for the difficulty of confronting these challenges theologically (but by no means the last word on the subject) is the understandable confusion about how to describe the chronic problem of obesity. Is it medical or moral? A sickness or a sin? Has the clinical discourse of addiction, compulsion, and dependence co-opted the biblical language of gluttony and lack of self-control?

Surely it's not an either-or proposition. Addictions are real and complicated and by definition not vanquished through willpower alone. But there *is* something about the thoroughgoing medicalization of contemporary life that makes it easy for Christians and Christian communities to cede authority (and sometimes our own best instincts) to medicine, psychotherapy, and pharmaceuticals. Often we defer to doctors because we are both bewildered and intimidated by a health care industry that regards human bodies as "potentially defective machines," in Wendell's Berry's memorable phrase.[31] This isolationist view of bodies and health—a highly paid specialist for this or that organ, for instance—typically regards obesity as an affliction of the autonomous patient-consumer to be treated increasingly with a choice of drugs or surgical procedures.

And thus we also sidestep much of our own culpability in eating too much. We know we shouldn't overindulge but we regard our routine proclivity to excess with a kind of amused resignation. With a shrug and a wink we reach for seconds, for another slice of pie or a fistful of cookies. Overeating during the "holidays" (now a continuous secular feast from late November till early January) becomes an opportunity for detailed reporting on epic binges and "turkey comas" on the couch. The sins of the body, our repressed Victorian ancestors insisted, are sexual not gastronomic, so our inability to control our desire for food is deemed regrettable weakness not grave sin. Gluttony—that ugly, old-fashioned word from Scripture—gets made over to refer to any number of vague appetites.

31. Berry, "Health Is Membership," 89.

The Eucharist and living eucharistically constitute an alternative to our fast-food culture of slow death. Obesity and malnutrition (often existing in the same family, even in the same person) are not mere "indicators" of poor health; they are a summons to the church to preach and to practice—always with humility and compassion—the salvation of the whole person.

Grace at the Table

A liturgically rooted response to the crisis of obesity insists, counterintuitively perhaps, that food is meant to be enjoyed and that meals ought to be occasions of extravagance and abundance. In the Eucharist, after all, we are invited to "taste and see that the Lord is good." And as we saw with the sacramental theology of the Wesleys, Holy Communion is a foretaste of the heavenly feast to come. Thus one "solution" to the problem of over-consumption is not deprivation—not endless scrimping and skimping and counting and calculating—but (re)discovering the pleasures of eating.[32] To take delight in good food mindfully prepared is to acknowledge our dependence on the abundant gifts of creation. As Wendell Berry contends,

> The pleasure of eating should be an *extensive* pleasure, not that of the mere gourmet. People who know the garden in which their vegetables have grown and know that the garden is healthy will remember the beauty of the growing plants, perhaps in the dewy first light of morning when gardens are at their best. Such a memory involves itself with the food and is one of the pleasures of eating. The knowledge of the good health of the garden relieves and frees and comforts the eater. . . . A significant part of the pleasure of eating is in one's accurate consciousness of the lives and the world from which food comes. The pleasure of eating, then, may be the best available standard of our health.[33]

To experience this pleasure, this *delight,* is to move beyond nourishment to conviviality. It is to consume our daily sustenance with the kind of attentive, unhurried gratitude (*eucharistia*) that the Lord's Supper summons us to.

In her exquisite short story "Babette's Feast" (and the stunning 1987 film version of it), Isak Dinesen tells the tale of Babette, a mysterious stranger who enters the lives of two reclusive sisters and the small, austere

---

32. The slow food movement has much to teach us here. See, for example, *Slow Food Nation*, by Carlo Petrini, and *Slow Food Revolution*, by Carlo Petrini and Gigi Padovani.

33. Berry, "Pleasures of Eating," 326. Berry's italics.

sect of Lutheran pietists they tend to in a remote region off the coast of Norway. Babette is a refugee of the French counterrevolution and, unbeknownst to this conservative community, a celebrated Parisian chef. After years of working as a maid for the sisters, preparing their staple meal of split cod and ale-bread soup, Babette wins the lottery and plans a lavish feast for the sisters and their neighbors who, by this point in the story, have become bitter and petty and fearful in their dealings with one another. Nervous about the upcoming banquet—especially as they notice cases of wine arriving along with a live turtle!—the sisters and the villagers determine to *endure* the sumptuous feast, not to enjoy it. For them, there is to be no pleasure in eating, or in much of anything else, it seems. On the night of the banquet, one of the guests is an army general—the son of one of the villagers and an old suitor of one of the sisters. As course after astonishing course is brought to the table, he recognizes the genius in their midst—and the unspeakable gift she has given her guests:

> In our human foolishness and short-sightedness we imagine that grace is finite. . . . But the moment comes when our eyes are opened and we realize that grace is infinite. Grace, my friends, demands nothing of us but that we shall await it with confidence and acknowledge it in gratitude. . . . Grace takes us all to its bosom and proclaims general amnesty. See! that which we have chosen is given us, and that which we have refused is, also and at the same time, granted us. Ay, that which we have rejected is poured upon us abundantly. For mercy and truth have met together, and righteousness and bliss have kissed one another![34]

After this remarkable speech, old grievances are addressed, old wounds healed. It was as if the rooms of the house, writes Dinesen, "had been filled with a heavenly light. . . . Taciturn old people received the gift of tongues; ears that for years had been almost deaf were opened to it. Time itself had merged into eternity."[35] The act of sharing an elaborate meal became a means of grace, a sacramental occasion for forgiveness and reconciliation and for experiencing beauty—the beauty of good food lovingly prepared, of friendships renewed, of food and wine and laughter around a table—as the theater of God's goodness and glory.

Yet perhaps all of this sounds a bit too pious and precious when what we're really craving is our favorite comfort food in the midst of our stressful

34. Dinesen, *Babette's Feast and Other Anecdotes of Destiny*, 40.

35. Ibid., 41.

lives. We are back to our old dilemma: we *know* we eat too much, want too much of the wrong kind of food, and are doing ourselves serious harm. Of course we need to eat less, exercise more, and learn to desire more healthful food. But we are trapped in habits of mind and body that make conversion difficult. We are by turns compulsive and careless in our eating; at times confident that we can do better (those earnest New Year's resolutions), at other times resigned to a life of endless struggle with food and weight and compromised health.

But if the Eucharist enacts the unity of the body, then we receive the gifts of bread and wine not as an aggregate of individuals but as those whose lives are linked through acts of mutual care and hospitality. My insecurities and anxieties about food are met by your willingness to be a source of support and encouragement and truth-telling to me, however tentative and clumsy our first attempts at this may be. The church's common witness to the bread that gives life, our drinking of the cup of salvation—these realities make sermons and studies and congregational conversations about food and health a natural and necessary outflow of eucharistic practice. An organic garden on church property or somewhere nearby becomes holy ground: fertile soil in which to grow not only food but friendships, a place where together we work out our salvation (*sōzō* = health, wholeness) with shovels and sweat (and a little fear and trembling), trusting that in due season we will indeed "taste and see that the Lord is good."

In describing the dual problem of overeating and obesity as not merely a lack of individual willpower but as a crisis of community—as a failure, even, of eucharistic imagination—we discover that we do not have to bear alone the burden of our destructive patterns of overconsumption. As we commune with sisters and brothers who experience the same struggles and setbacks, our food-related pathologies are received with compassion and understanding at the table of grace.

At the same time, though, we acknowledge that a preoccupation with our own food-related failures can keep us from a true catholicity, from recognizing that in every local assembly is gathered the transglobal body of Christ. In fellowship and responsibility we are joined to these sisters and brothers far and near. Therefore at the Lord's Table we confess our complicity with an industrial food system that contributes not only to our own poor health but to that of our neighbors and the planet. As fast food has gone global, previously unexperienced health crises are emerging around the world. U.S. agricultural policy, with its heavy crop subsidies (mainly corn), has meant the underwriting of chronic obesity in those who are forced to subsist on cheap, processed, overly sweetened foods.

Yet through the gifts of bread and wine our lives are linked to theirs: "When one member suffers, all suffer together with it" (1 Cor 12:26). At every local celebration of the Lord's Supper is the welcome intrusion of the universal body of Christ, and the work of justice flows outward from the Table to the neighbor in need. This meal is the revolutionary witness to the health and well-being—the *shalom* of God—that is creation's true end. The Eucharist, as the Wesleys well knew, marks the intersection of what has been with what will be.

In the mid-1990s, Sara Miles—a leftist journalist with no experience of church life—impulsively walked into an Episcopal church in San Francisco and received the sacrament of Holy Communion. "It changed everything," she writes in her memoir, *Take This Bread*.[36] In the months and years that followed, Miles organized food pantries around the city, the first one distributing thousands of pounds of fruit and vegetables and cereal every week around the same altar where Miles first ate the bread of the Eucharist. The intersection of food and bodies had always interested her—as a restaurant cook, a war correspondent in Latin America, a political activist in California—but in that first impetuous taste of consecrated bread and wine, Miles discovered herself to be part of something "huger and wider" than she had ever expected: "the suffering, fractious, unboundaried body of Christ."[37]

> [The gospel] proclaims against reason that the hungry will be fed, that those cast down will be raised up, and that all things, including my own failures, are being made new. It offers food without exception to the worthy and unworthy, the screwed up and pious, and then commands everyone to do the same. It doesn't promise to solve or erase suffering but to transform it, pledging that by loving one another, even through pain, we will find more life. And it insists that by opening ourselves to strangers, the despised or frightening or unintelligible other, we will see more and more of the holy, since, without exception, all people are one body: God's.[38]

36. Miles, *Take This Bread*, xi.

37. Ibid., xv.

38. Ibid., xvi.

Summary

"Food is the daily sacrament of unnecessary goodness," observes Episcopal priest and chef Robert Farrar Capon. Tomato sandwiches and church supper casseroles and urban food pantries are material evidence of the sheer gratuity of creation. In the Eucharist—also a sign of superfluous abundance—we receive even our own lives as gifts and learn that the whole of creation lives from the inexhaustible generosity of God.

It is a modest meal—a bit of bread, a sip of wine or juice. But in and through it are possibilities for transformed living. With thanksgiving we eat and drink, Sunday and every day, to the health of our bodies, our neighbors' bodies, and our world.

Questions for Consideration

1. What are some of the cultural contradictions that inform and affect the way we understand health and happiness?

   a. What are some of the problems the church has inherited from the Greek view of the human person? How does such a view contribute to the "devaluing" of creation, of the body?

   b. How does the definition of happiness as "becoming more like God in goodness" help provide a resource for cultivating practices of health and well-being?

   c. How can the "constant duty" of sharing in the Eucharist inform the way we as Christians are to think and act regarding health, happiness, and the good life?

2. What were some of John Wesley's attitudes and practices regarding health and its relation to happiness?

3. What importance did the Eucharist have in the Wesleyan movement?

4. How does the eschatological emphasis on the Eucharist that the Wesley brothers articulated point to the holistic dimension of the gospel, or to the fullness of God's shalom, and the communal-social aspects of the Christian life?

5. How did John Wesley's penchant for discipline and method and accountability in the "societies" and class meetings speak to the early Methodists' striving for health and well-being? How may images of "kitchen-gathering" or "bread-baking" assist Christians today in practicing God's shalom? What links between Eucharist and health may we want to make today that the Wesley brothers didn't make between Eucharist and health?

6. What are the ways in which we can begin to see the connection between the Eucharist and urgent ongoing questions about food production and distribution?

   a. What are the theological and political "dots" we need to connect with respect to the Eucharist and the God who "links food with justice"?

b. How does the radical individualism of much modern Christianity train us to overlook the connections between the practice of our faith and the practices of eating and food consumption? Explain.

c. What are some of the ways in which the church today may need to rethink what it means to "eat together," especially as that pertains to potlucks, clergy health, physical appearance, and societal matters such as the relation of race and class to poor health?

7. How might "saying grace" at the table move us to share gratitude as a way of "slowing down"?

a. How are overeating, obesity, and other problems regarding food distribution and consumption a failure of the community rather than of the individual? How do these problems reveal a failure of our eucharistic imagination? Share examples.

b. How does the Eucharist mark the intersection of what has been and what will be, what is shared and what is not, what is our true end and what is not? Share.

c. What theological resources might the eucharistic hymns of Charles Wesley offer in the renewal of our imaginations as they pertain to health, both spiritual and physical?

three

Beauty: The Christian Life and the Pursuit of Perfection

Part of what it means to be, is to be beautiful. Beauty is not superadded to things; it is one of the springs of their reality.

—Francesca Murphy, *Christ the Form of Beauty*

The beauty of holiness, of that inward man of the heart which is renewed after the image of God, cannot but strike every eye which God hath opened, every enlightened understanding.

—John Wesley, "Upon Our Lord's Sermon on the Mount, Discourse IV"

Why do you trouble her? She has done a beautiful thing for me.

—Mark 14:6 ESV

Beauty Shop

The juxtaposition of "health and beauty" in the title of this book is meant in part to conjure the ways these terms often go together in contemporary culture. Consider, for example, the "health and beauty" aisle of the local discount store, with its bewildering assortment of pharmaceuticals and cosmetics, everything from cold medicine to cold cream, diet pills to nail polish, sunscreen to "bronzing" lotion. This ubiquitous and unquestioned arrangement seems to suggest that we are healthy, we are beautiful—and thus we are happy—insofar as we are able to purchase the products that promise to deliver these desired states of being.

Beauty in the popular imagination and in a capitalist economy is an "industry" before it is anything else, a complex of products and regimens ingeniously packaged, marketed, and sold to anxious consumers. Like impossible thinness, our culture worships and promotes a standard of beauty founded on a fiction: perpetual youth and the flawlessness (and vigorous health) we associate with it. In this, the quest to be beautiful is the pursuit of perfection—perfect skin, perfect hair, perfect teeth, perfect body. As we noted in chapter 2, even when we concede the futility of such a quest, the ideal itself holds powerful sway over how we regard ourselves and those around us.

In other arenas of contemporary life, beauty is also equated with what is pretty and pleasing to the eye, to the exclusion of what is flawed, broken, tainted, and decidedly not perfect. We rightly marvel at a stunning sunset but do not quite know how to locate such beauty within the processes of nature that give us, say, cyclones and tsunamis. The enormously popular art of Thomas Kinkade, the "painter of light," feeds our hunger for homey perfection—tidy cottages and gardens, churches and fields and flowing streams, all bathed in a soft, golden glow that keeps from view the blemishes and defects of real places and the people who inhabit them. We might say that such art misrepresents reality by promoting a kind of false innocence—that it is sentimental kitsch.[1] But, again, even a false ideal, whether of the perfect body or the perfect flowerbed, exerts tremendous power over our individual and collective conceptions of beauty.

In this chapter we will take up the subjects of beauty and perfection by first expanding our understandings of each. In classical thought, beauty had to do fundamentally with what is *fitting, properly ordered, proportionate, in harmony or agreement, consonant in its parts.* One way that Christian

---

1. Jeremy Begbie argues that the sentimentalist misrepresents reality through evading or trivializing evil and is emotionally self-indulgent. He quotes Milan Kundera's well-known definition of kitsch: "Kitsch causes two tears to flow in quick succession. The first tear says: how nice to see children running on the grass! The second tear says: how nice to be moved, together with all mankind, by children running on the grass! It is the second tear that makes kitsch kitsch." Begbie, "Beauty and Sentimentality in the Arts," 50.

theology has spoken of beauty is by recognizing and naming a fittingness or consonance between God's trinitarian life of generosity and ceaseless love and our own lives, personally and corporately lived in and for the world—even when such harmony or agreement is only fleetingly glimpsed or experienced. Perfection, similarly, is not about flawlessness, though for a time John Wesley would insist on the real possibility of sinlessness. Rather, perfection, as we will see, names a disposition of benevolence that is characteristic of God's nature, God's beauty—a nature and a beauty in which we, as participants in the divine life, have a share.

Beauty in Christian Theology

From the Greek philosophers Christianity borrowed the language of the *transcendentals*: universal properties of being variously described by the ancients as unity, truth, goodness, wisdom, beauty, and justice, all of which were thought to characterize everything that exists in the world. Atoms and daisies and persons and prime numbers—*all things*—participate in being, have a common "is-ness," we might say, before they are distinguishable as objects or entities. The early Christian tradition, in reflecting on God as perfect being, settled on the transcendentals of *truth, goodness, and beauty*, the properties that God was believed to possess in infinite abundance and that everything which exists, by virtue of its existence, has a share in. These properties or determinations of being indwell one another; they are, in a sense, interchangeable, indivisibly one, such that the *true*, we could say, is also always *good* and *beautiful*.

St. Augustine gave a particular kind of attention to these matters in the fifth century, as did St. Thomas Aquinas in the thirteenth century and Hans Urs von Balthasar in the twentieth. Balthasar was especially keen to recover beauty as a corrective to the state of modern theology in which "there is no longer any space for wonder at the fact that there is something rather than nothing."[2] For this Swiss Catholic theologian, beauty is the sister to truth and goodness that we banish at our peril. "We can be sure," warns Balthasar, "that whoever sneers at [beauty's] name, as if she were the ornament of a bourgeois past, whether he admits it or not, can no longer pray and soon will no longer be able to love."[3]

2. Balthasar, *Glory of the Lord*, 5:613.
3. Ibid., 1:18.

For Balthasar, a Christian account of beauty is rooted in the triunity of God and in the revelation of the triune God's *glory* in history. God's glory, which we might speak of as the radiance of God's perfect, self-giving love, or the light of divine mutual indwelling that draws all things to itself, is materially mediated. It is not abstract, theoretical, ephemeral. "No metaphysics of Being," Balthasar contends, "can be separated from concrete experience."[4] God's glory, the divine beauty, makes itself known in *form*, a term central to Balthasar's entire project. The form above all forms that reveals the beauty of God is Jesus Christ: his life and teaching, and also and especially his suffering, death, and resurrection. "The beauty of Christ," Francesca Murphy notes in her reading of Balthasar, "is not that of a luminous icon, crystallized into immobile perfection. It is the beauty of an action."[5] The beauty of the triune God, we might say, is given shape and substance—is *performed* for us—in the life and ministry, the torture and execution, the resurrection and ascension of Jesus of Nazareth. But not only that. In manifesting this beauty of the triune God, Christ summons *us* to action, to mission, to participation with God in the mending of the world—to *be beautiful*. Thus, *beauty* is an inescapable category for thinking about everything from creation to crucifixion to Christian discipleship—*and* for living into the fullness of the love and communion we were created for.

But for all that Balthasar assumes about the centrality of beauty, the modern era has not been so enthusiastic. By the eighteenth and nineteenth centuries, a distinction between objective and subjective truth was firmly in place, with beauty reduced to a matter of preference, sentiment, and subjective taste ("beauty is in the eye of the beholder"). Most philosophers and theologians considered beauty anything *but* an inescapable category for their work and were, in fact, deeply suspicious of beauty since it was deemed incapable of meeting the rigorous truth claims of Christian teaching. Especially since the Enlightenment, with that era's championing of rationalization, industrialization, and bureaucratization, the *beautiful* has all but disappeared as a means for thinking about and describing and, most importantly, *living* the Christian life. Much of modern theology, as Balthasar lamented, surrendered beauty to a propositional view of the faith—Christianity as a catalog of concepts, a laundry list of truth claims to be assented to with the rational mind.[6]

4. Balthasar, "Transcendentality and Gestalt," 29.
5. Murphy, *Christ the Form of Beauty*, 146.
6. See my essay "'Beautiful and Pointless': Poetry and the Theological Task."

Another concern raised by modern thinkers, mindful of the world's darkness and ugliness, is the seeming incongruity between beauty and evil, beauty and suffering, beauty and death. Yet St. Augustine championed their continuity, indeed, their intimate connection: "The deformity of Christ forms you. For if he had not wished to be deformed you would not have received back the form that you lost. Therefore, he hung deformed upon the cross, but his deformity was our beauty."[7] This arresting imagery jars our modern sensibilities; the torture and death of Jesus is the epitome of *ugliness*, so goes the understandable protest. And with our contemporary notions of beauty so narrowly defined, Augustine's words might also seem to encourage the tendency to associate the crucifixion with sentimentality and affect and emotional self-indulgence—to regard its import as a matter of private devotion rather than as costly action. But perhaps most of our discomfort arises from the sense that a description like Augustine's (and the notion of beauty it undergirds) seems not to reckon seriously enough with profound moral evil. All this talk of beauty in the face of incalculable anguish and affliction—where does that get us in a Holocaust-haunted world? How does beauty take sober, sufficient account of suffering bodies?

One final obstacle to a robust recovery of beauty for Christian living is the view that beauty is fundamentally utilitarian in nature. For centuries the Christian tradition has inspired and cultivated beauty in its art, architecture, liturgy, and music. The Sistine Chapel, Rembrandt's *Return of the Prodigal Son*, Dante's *Divine Comedy*, Gregorian chant, the hymns of Charles Wesley—these and thousands of other expressions of the sublime are enduring testaments to the human imagination's longing to communicate in artistic form something of the splendor and glory of God. But the modern stance toward such beauty has been preoccupied with concerns like these: What *good* do these beautiful objects do? How should we make *use* of them? Does this kind of beauty demand anything more than *appreciation*? These are not unimportant questions, but they are not the same as this chapter's foundational one: *How is the Christian life itself beautiful?* If we participate in beauty by virtue of our createdness, our very *being*, and if "beauty is reality under the aspect of form,"[8] then our task (and our joy) is not to *possess* beauty but to understand how beauty possesses us—how beauty is at the heart of what it means to be human.

---

7. *Sermo* 27.6, quoted in Sherry, *Spirit and Beauty*, 74.

8. Murphy, *Christ the Form of Beauty*, 31.

Since Balthasar's ground-breaking work, a wealth of scholarship has been produced that aims to recover the necessity—the utter centrality—of beauty for Christian theology and discipleship. As we will see, contemporary theologians like Francesca Murphy and David Bentley Hart write compellingly about the beautiful. But the great majority of Christian thinkers have kept their distance from beauty, either disregarding it completely or regarding it with deep suspicion. The Protestant Reformation that shaped the theological world of the Wesleys was responsible for much of this stance toward beauty.

A Contradiction in Terms

Protestant aesthetic.

There are reasons—especially in this era of church growth, capital campaigns, and the praise and worship team—why these words do not seem to go together in the popular imagination. When Martin Luther and John Calvin undertook church reform in their respective parts of Europe in the sixteenth century, neither intended at the outset to launch the movement we now know as Protestantism. This would also be the case some two hundred years later when the brothers Wesley sought to renew the Anglican Church; they had no designs on establishing for the ages something called—pejoratively by their peers—"Methodism." But Reformation theology spread quickly, thanks in large part to the timely invention of moveable type. Johannes Gutenberg's printing press hastened the break with Rome in churches across western Europe by making it possible to get documents of protest into the hands of would-be dissenters. But the printing press was also quite literally a sign for what the Reformation, broadly conceived and carried out, sought to champion—*the written word*—and what it was generally suspicious of—*image* and *adornment*.

The Reformers did not employ the language of the transcendentals, but *truth* was much more on their minds than was *beauty* or even *goodness*. There are notable exceptions to this, even in the writings of Luther and Calvin. Both were convinced, for instance, of the glory of the material world. For Calvin, especially, whose popular reputation through the centuries has hardened unfairly into that of a dour judge eager to consign the reprobate to eternal damnation, a passage like this from his seminal work is striking: "Since the perfection of blessedness consists in the knowledge of God, he has been pleased, in order that none might be excluded from the means of obtaining felicity, not only to deposit in our minds that seed of religion of which we have already spoken, but so to manifest his perfections in the whole structure of the universe, and daily place himself in our view, that we cannot open our eyes without being compelled to behold him."[9] Our difficulty in beholding God in this way, our *sin*, Calvin might say, is poor vision or distorted perception. We cannot see clearly the divine "perfections" (Calvin's nod, perhaps, to the unity of truth, goodness, and beauty?) that figure forth from the material order. Yet for this French humanist and church reformer they are always there nonetheless. As the theater of God's glory, creation is sustained by God's presence, and, as Jeremy Begbie puts it, "God testifies to his own beauty through creation's own beauty."[10]

The eighteenth-century composer Johann Sebastian Bach, schooled in Lutheran theology (having learned Latin, Bible history, the catechism, and how to chant the Psalms), also breaks the stereotype about Protestantism and beauty. Orthodox theologian David Bentley Hart calls Bach "the greatest of theologians, the most inspired witness to the *ordo amoris* [order of love] in the fabric of being."[11] In the aftermath of resigning a church organist position due to theological disagreements with its Pietist pastor, Bach wrote wistfully, "I should always have liked to work toward the goal, namely, of a well-regulated church music, to the glory of God."[12] Bach was an orderly, systematic composer, the master of the ultra-rational fugal form, and yet he created sublimely, searingly beautiful works that enrapture the heart and soul. In Bach's music, says Hart, is a vision of order—order within difference, order within beauty—that no theologian has ever been capable of putting into words.[13] This vision of order encompasses the dif-

9. Calvin, *Institutes of the Christian Religion*. Marilynne Robinson has perhaps done more than anyone to rehabilitate Calvin's reputation in both her critical essays and her fiction. Here is a beautiful example from her novel *Gilead*—an insight/observation voiced by the book's central character, an aging Congregationalist pastor: "Calvin says somewhere that each of us is an actor on a stage and God is the audience. That metaphor has always interested me, because it makes us artists of our behavior, and the reaction of God to us might be thought of as aesthetic rather than morally judgmental in the ordinary sense. . . . I suppose Calvin's God was a Frenchman, just as mine is a Middle Westerner of New England extraction. Well, we all bring such light to bear on these great matters as we can. I do like Calvin's image, though, because it suggests how God might actually enjoy us. I believe we think about that far too little" (124).

10. Begbie, "Created Beauty," 25.

11. Hart, *Beauty of the Infinite*, 282.

12. David and Mendel, *Bach Reader*, 60.

13. Hart, *Beauty of the Infinite*, 282. I am grateful to my friend Alison Anderson for

ference that is intrinsic to unity—in great music, in the order of creation, in the triune God. Indeed, Bach's genius for improvisation—for music that is "astonishingly contingent, free of necessity"—conjures a vision of God's beauty as "the particularizing, proliferating ministry of the Holy Spirit, effecting faithful but unpredictable improvisations on the harmony achieved in Jesus Christ."[14]

Another figure from the eighteenth century who may surprise with his attention to beauty: New England churchman Jonathan Edwards, born the same year as John Wesley. The Puritanism associated with Edwards, like the later Calvinism attributed to John Calvin, distorts and reduces the complexity of Edwards's vast theological output. For those who may know his most famous sermon "Sinners in the Hands of an Angry God," with its anxiety-producing sternness and lurid fascination with hell, there is also Edwards's lifelong insistence that "God is God, and distinguished from all other beings, and exalted above 'em, chiefly by his divine beauty."[15] Edwards wrote extensively on the Trinity as a society of love and beauty, insisting that God's beauty is "the highest form of primary beauty or loving consent and consists of the most complex form of relationality."[16] Edwards rarely used the classical Greek terms for describing the nature of God as triune (*ousia*, or substance, for instance), preferring instead words like "delight." And he wrote regularly of God's dynamic "disposition" toward communicative love.[17] For Edwards, God is not a static entity but beauty in action, creating the world out of an overflowing generosity and fecundity of God's own being. As theologian Belden Lane has noted, Edwards prefigures Balthasar when he writes that "[beauty] is what we are concerned with more than anything else."[18]

In the twentieth century the great Swiss theologian Karl Barth gave attention to the concept of beauty, even if he was reluctant to ascribe beauty to God. According to Barth, "God is not beautiful in the sense that he shares in an idea of beauty superior to him, so that to know it is to know

---

broadening my understanding of Bach's genius for improvisation within order, difference within unity.

14. Begbie, "Created Beauty," 38.

15. Edwards, *Religious Affections*, 298.

16. McDermott, *Understanding Jonathan Edwards*, 114.

17. Lee, *Philosophical Theology of Jonathan Edwards*, 5.

18. Lane, "Jonathan Edwards on Beauty," 48. Lane notes that George Marsden, in his biography of Edwards, contends that "the key to Edwards' thought is that everything is related because everything is related to God," 44.

him as God. On the contrary, it is as he is God that he is also beautiful, so that he is the basis and standard of everything that is beautiful and of all ideas of the beautiful."[19] Where Balthasar saw beauty as constitutive of God's glory, Barth (who shared a friendship with his Catholic counterpart) believed beauty to be secondary to the glory of God.[20] Still, Barth stands in a line—albeit a short one—of Protestant thinkers and theologians who gave attention to beauty within the framework of Christian doctrine.

Yet those in this line, as we have said, are the notable exceptions. Protestantism generally and the Reformed tradition particularly have been more concerned with dogmatic truth and moral rigor than with beauty. (Though, again, the *unity* of truth, goodness, and beauty reveal these to be arbitrary distinctions.) While Luther regarded the Word of God as pluriform and dynamic (written text and divine *Logos* and the act and art of preaching all at once), a distinctive feature of the Protestantism that came after him was (and is) a kind of singular fixation on the Bible—read, proclaimed, and responded to as an act of the individual will and intellect.[21] What matters for the Christian life within such a framework is that one adheres to Scripture's precepts—extractable rules and norms intended to govern one's behavior before an all-knowing, all-seeing, all-powerful God. And while biblical interpreters before the modern era often took note of (and delighted in) the *beauty* of Scripture, especially in regard to the multiple meanings it yielded, heirs of the Reformation (who were also, of course, heirs of the Enlightenment) often "flattened" the words of the Bible, wringing from them multiplicity and fluidity, and imposing a rigid uniformity on words and ideas whose beauty (and strangeness) are essential in shaping discipleship and Christian witness.[22]

Protestantism's emphasis on the written word also had the effect of rendering the *visual*—the imagistic, the iconic—suspect. Art, *per se*, was not rejected. Calvin, for instance, believed that all great art ultimately comes from God and that the gift of artistic expression sometimes flourishes most brilliantly in nonbelievers.[23] Later Reformers, including many of

19. Barth, *Church Dogmatics* II/1, 656.

20. Begbie notes that Barth's concerns in this debate are methodological—that the Swiss Reformer did not want beauty to be a "leading concept" in the doctrine of God. Such concerns, says Begbie, ought to be seriously heeded ("Created Beauty," 21).

21. For a nuanced treatment of Luther's views in Luther's context, see Senn, *Christian Liturgy*.

22. Murphy, "'Beautiful and Pointless': Poetry and the Theological Task."

23. De Gruchy, "Holy Beauty," 20.

the Puritans, did not object to art in secular spaces or even to religious art in the public square. What they protested, as John de Gruchy points out, was the presence of images, icons, or other artistic objects in the worship space—"ostentation and adornment that distracted from the dignity and simplicity of true worship and therefore authentic Christian living."[24]

The Old Testament's prohibition against graven images served as justification for some Protestant communities to rid their worship spaces of sculptures and paintings, though this did not develop uniformly across Protestantism.[25] Lutheran architecture, for instance, in the decades after Luther's break with Rome, retained altars, candles, crucifixes, vestments, and organs. In England, under Queen Elizabeth I, roods—the large crucifixes of medieval churches often mounted on elaborate "screens" and placed at the chancel entrance—were destroyed. When the need arose for new church buildings in the seventeenth century, due to destruction during the Thirty Years' War or fire or the growth of cities, the new architecture reflected a basic requirement of Protestant worship: a high and visible pulpit for the preaching and hearing of the word. Altars were not unimportant and churches experimented with their placement (in Scotland, communicants sat around tables placed in the aisles), but making the pulpit visible and the preacher audible were of paramount importance. To that end, galleries were sometimes installed, many of them multitiered like theater seats, so that people could better see and hear.

When the Puritans began constructing churches in America, their simple "meeting houses" reflected the influence of Sir Christopher Wren, who had built some fifty churches in London after the fire of 1666. His "auditory" church plans, featuring a one-room hall design, were derived from his own calculations of how close worshipers needed to be to a pulpit in order to "hear distinctly," and the pews in Wren's churches always faced the direction of the pulpit, not the altar.[26] While the architecture of America's

24. Ibid. De Gruchy goes on to say that, with Calvin, the Puritans objected "to any attempt by artists to usurp the role of God as creator" (20).

25. Senn offers a richly detailed account of these matters; see his *Christian Liturgy*, especially 529–33. My brief sketch here draws on his lively and informative narrative.

26. Senn shares some informative and entertaining details about church pews, noting that the enclosed, high-back bench pews of the Protestant churches of this era were designed for practical reasons, like "keep[ing] out drafts of wind when the doors were opened." "In the winter," he reports, "footwarmers were placed in them to keep worshipers warm, and they served as 'play pens' for small children during the service. The high backs cut down the view of objects or other worshipers, but this was considered reinforcement to meditation. . . . Wren himself would have liked to be rid of pews, but

city churches in the colonial period varied for many reasons—denomina-tional affiliation, wealth, and patronage (or a lack of it)—the churches of the frontier were almost always simple and plain, stark even, in their aesthetic. Pews and a pulpit (and maybe a woodburning stove for warmth) were all that were needed for the word of God to be duly preached and heard.

The Wesleys on Beauty

Preaching the word of God was a task that John Wesley undertook with great seriousness and boundless energy. A lifelong Anglican, Wesley was both a duly ordained priest of the state church and a self-appointed field evangelist. He was a classically educated Oxford don and an itinerant revivalist with Pietist leanings.[27] This lifelong tension reveals itself in a number of ways in Wesley's writings, but in his few, brief, and scattered observations on beauty—both on works of art and on the grandeur of the natural world—we see the balance tip toward the Pietist strain in Wesley's worldview.

In observations meticulously recorded in his journal and in some brief remarks on the nature of taste, Wesley offers glimpses of a way of beholding the world—of naming and describing the works of creation, human nature, the way of salvation—that reflects a belief in the clear separation between the sacred and the profane. He is not unusual in this. In fact, recalling our discussion of dualism in chapter 2, Wesley was typical of his era in that he worked within the inherited binaries of body and soul, matter and spirit, nature and supernature. He was not of course a Gnostic (one who denies or denigrates the material realm), but Wesley set the sacred and profane in uneasy opposition to each other.

In the early 1970s Orthodox priest and theologian Alexander Schme-mann noted how unbiblical the sacred/profane divide is and how the

---

church leaders preferred to keep them as a source of income (they were rented or sold); and worshipers appreciated the fact that they kept out the draft" (*Christian Liturgy*, 533).

27. "Pietism" names a movement within Protestantism first associated with the seventeenth-century German reformer Philipp Jakob Spener. His proposals for church renewal included the rigorous study of the Bible by laypeople in small groups and a plain style of preaching meant to edify and transform the hearer (and to counter pulpit oratory that flaunted the rhetorical skills of the preacher). Wesley's first—and life-changing—en-counter with Moravian Pietists occurred on his voyage to the Georgia Colony in 1735. He was also profoundly affected by the counsel and lifelong friendship of Pietist pastor and bishop Peter Böhler.

early church understood the whole created order as a "cosmic sacrament," as divine gift received, blessed, and returned to God as human beings—priests of creation—commune with Christ and make God known in the world.[28] For Schmemann, we live between two *ages*—time fallen and time redeemed—but there is no *spatial* dimension that is not infused with God's presence and power (and thus God's beauty).

This is not John Wesley's view of things, but we will see that there are ways to read the early Methodist tradition that open up possibilities for a Wesleyan understanding of beauty that the Wesleys themselves did not necessarily aspire to.

But, first, a few of John's observations on beauty.

Scattered among the journal entries that chronicle Wesley's travels and his preaching engagements (he logged a quarter-million miles and gave some forty thousand sermons) are descriptions of his encounters with various works of art, architecture, scenes of natural beauty, and sometimes artists themselves. The general tone of these observations is one of admiration mixed with admonishment—a warning, of sorts, that objects of beauty and the artists who create them may provide moments of sensory pleasure but they will ultimately disappoint. Art and beauty are of the material realm and, as such, in Wesley's estimation, fleeting, even trifling. What endures, and what must be attended to diligently and steadfastly, is what transpires in the realm of the spirit: the working out of one's salvation and the calm assurance of it—an honest and sober reckoning with the true state of one's soul.

One example of Wesley's way of both praising and condemning a work of art is found in an entry he wrote in February 1772 after a visit to Hampton Court, where he viewed *The Holy Family with Saints Elizabeth and John the Baptist*, by the prominent Flemish painter Peter Paul Rubens. (Rubens painted several versions of this scene between 1610 and 1620.) One wonders if Wesley intended the irony (and humor) of his opening sentence since immediately after it he launches into a typically robust critique of an unfamiliar work of art: "Of pictures I do not pretend to be a judge; but there is one, by Paul Rubens, which particularly struck me, both with the design and the execution of it. It is Zacharias and Elisabeth, with John the Baptist, two or three years old, coming to visit Mary, and our Lord sitting upon her knee. The passions are surprisingly expressed, even in the children; but I could not see either the decency or common sense of painting them stark

28. Schmemann, *For the Life of the World*.

naked. Nothing can defend or excuse this; it is shockingly absurd, even an Indian being the judge. I allow, a man who paints thus may have a good hand but *cerebrum non habet* [he has no brain]."[29]

In many ways, Wesley's response reveals well-known qualities of his character (and of his era): modesty, propriety, and a fastidiousness in how one engages the unfamiliar and unsettling. (His backhanded racism—"even an Indian being the judge"—is also, alas, typical of the times). And we should not expect John Wesley—Anglican clergyman, itinerant field preacher—to be a savvy art critic. As British musicologist Erik Routley has observed about Wesley, "his judgments [about art and music] were technically naïve, temperamentally characteristic of the culture from which he came."[30] Yet they also highlight a foundational theological conviction of Wesley's: art and beauty occupy a plane of existence distinct from that where vital piety—love of God and neighbor—is nurtured and practiced. And in holding to such a conviction Wesley also reveals a telling sensibility about the material realm: one keeps one's distance from—and refuses to be moved or transported (or rendered silent) by—great art. In this vein, while in Cologne, Germany, in the summer of 1738, not long after his conversion experience in Aldersgate Street, London, Wesley made this dismissive observation: "We went to the cathedral, which is mere heaps upon heaps; a huge mis-shapen thing, which has no more of symmetry than of neatness belonging to it."[31]

Wesley did believe, however, that poetry could sometimes be instructive—that it had the potential to serve as a kind of "handmaid of piety."[32] He is uncharacteristically effusive about Homer's *Odyssey* in a journal entry from September 1769—*after* voicing some customary complaints:

> Last week I read over, as I rode, [a] great part of Homer's *Odyssey*. I always imagined it was, like Milton's *Paradise Regained*, the last faint effort of an expiring muse. But how was I mistaken! How far has Homer's latter poem the pre-eminence over the former! It is not, indeed, without its blemishes; among which, perhaps, one might reckon his making Ulysses swim nine days and nine nights without sustenance; the incredible manner of his escape

29. Wesley, *Journal*, 5:444.

30. Routley, *Musical Wesleys*, 25.

31. Wesley, *Journal*, 2:8.

32. This phrase comes from Wesley's preface to the 1780 edition of *Hymns for the People Called Methodist*: "When poetry thus keeps its place as the handmaid of piety, it shall attain, not a poor perishable wealth, but a crown that fadeth not away."

from Polyphemus (unless the goat was as strong as an ox), and the introducing Minerva at every turn, without any *dignus vindice nodus*. But his numerous beauties make large amends for these. Was ever man so happy in his descriptions, so exact and consistent in his characters, and so natural in telling a story? He likewise continually inserts the finest strokes of morality (which I cannot find in Virgil); on all occasions recommending the fear of God, with justice, mercy, and truth. In this only he is inconsistent with himself: he makes his hero say:

> Wisdom never lies;

And

> Him, on whate'er pretence, that lies can tell,
> My soul abhors him as the gates of hell.

Meantime, he himself, on the slightest pretence, tells deliberate lies over and over; nay, and is highly commended for so doing, even by the Goddess of Wisdom![33]

Here Wesley reveals a kind of delight and playfulness that is often absent in his reflections on art and beauty. And he offers a firsthand glimpse of something known about his extensive travels: Wesley often read philosophy, history, literature, and poetry while riding horseback. One imagines Wesley—the serious Pietist, the earnest evangelist—lost in wonder for long stretches of time as he absorbed the tales of the traveler Odysseus on his own long and arduous journeys.

In a final example from Wesley's journal we again see admiration turn to admonishment. In May 1774 he wrote,

After preaching at Cockermouth and Wigton, I went on to Carlisle and preached to a very serious congregation. Here I saw a very extraordinary genius, a man blind from four years of age, who could wind worsted, weave flowered plush on an engine and loom of his own making; who wove his own name in plush, and made his own clothes and his own tools of every sort. Some years ago, being shut up in the organ loft at church, he felt every part of it and afterward made an organ for himself which, judges say, is an exceedingly good one. He then taught himself to play upon it psalm tunes, anthems, voluntaries, or anything which he heard. I heard him play several tunes with great accuracy, and a complex voluntary. I suppose all Europe can hardly produce such another

---

33. Wesley, *Journal*, 5:339–40. *Dignus vindice nodus* is a phrase from antiquity meaning a difficulty (knot) worthy of a (divine) deliverer.

instance. His name is Joseph Strong. But what is he the better for all this if he is still "without God in the world"?[34]

For Wesley, beauty is not in the *beingness* of things. He does not operate with the assumption that everything that exists has a share in the good, the true, and the beautiful since to *be* is to be these things. For him, beauty is not an objective property of being but a category of human experience or human making. In this he keeps company with a long line of Enlightenment philosophers on the subject, including Descartes, Hume, Locke, and Kant. But Wesley also makes the *theological* move, as we see here in his observations on Joseph Strong, of opposing beauty to Christian faith, or at least of separating it from the realm of what is considered sacred or holy—the realm in which piety is practiced and salvation secured. Sadly, Wesley cannot imagine that the blind artist he encountered in his travels in northwest England somehow *bears* in his art and in his being the beauty, truth, and goodness of God.

In some brief reflections on the topic of taste, Wesley again adheres to the philosophical tradition to which he is heir. When late medieval and early modern thinkers shifted the discourse of beauty from the objective to the subjective, from the idea that beauty inheres in all things to the belief that beauty resides in the realm of the passions and dispositions, the problem of *taste* arose. Interestingly, Enlightenment thinkers like David Hume employed the term "taste" as a hedge against the complete subjectification of beauty, hoping to rescue it from what it would eventually become: "a term for the arbitrary aesthetic preferences of individuals."[35] We know this more colloquially by the phrase "beauty is in the eye of the beholder." Wesley drew on the writing of eighteenth-century essayist and poet Joseph Addison to distinguish between "dull taste" and "a good, a just, or a true taste." The former is "faint and languid . . . [and] has no lively perception of its object."[36] According to Wesley, dull taste gravitates toward "low compositions in music or poetry, or coarse and worthless pictures."[37] The latter, he insists, is evident in one "who discerns and relishes whatever, either in the works of nature or of art, is truly excellent in its kind."[38] Good taste (or also "correct taste" or "fine taste") is something one is born with—although,

34. Ibid., 6:104–5.
35. Farley, *Faith and Beauty*, 35.
36. Wesley, "Thoughts Upon Taste," 468.
37. Ibid.
38. Ibid.

quoting Addison, Wesley notes that there are several means of improving it, the most natural of which is "to be conversant with the writings of the best authors."[39]

Yet Wesley makes a surprising (and beautiful) turn when he ponders whether there is—alongside a taste for flowers, meadows, painting, or poetry—"a kind of internal sense, whereby we relish the happiness of our fellow-creatures, even without any reflection on our own interest, without any reference to ourselves? whereby we bear a part in the prosperity of others, and rejoice with them that rejoice? Surely there is something still in the human mind, in many, if not in all, (whether by nature, or from a higher principle), which interests us in the welfare, not only of our relatives, our friends, and our neighbours, but of those who are at the greatest distance from us, whether in time or place. And the most generous minds have most of this taste for human happiness."[40] He goes on to observe that "there is a beauty in virtue, in gratitude, and disinterested benevolence. . . . And is not this pleasure [the taste for this kind of beauty] infinitely more delicate, than any that ever resulted, yea, or can result, from the utmost refinements of music, poetry, or painting?"[41] While we see Wesley still operating with perhaps too clear a division between the sacred and profane, he does open up the possibility of locating beauty within lived discipleship, within the practice of the love of God and neighbor that constitutes the sum of the Christian life. Wesley works out the particulars of these insights, of this "taste for human happiness," in his notion of Christian perfection. And it is in this neglected and often misunderstood doctrine that the contours of a Wesleyan aesthetic begin to show themselves.

On Christian Perfection

To examine the Wesleyan doctrine of perfection and its connections to beauty, it is instructive to look briefly at some of the hymns of John's brother, Charles, who often stands in the shadows when the story of Methodism is

---

39. Ibid. It is worth noting, yet beyond the scope of our purposes here to pursue, that these views on taste and beauty, developed by Addison and his contemporaries and endorsed fairly whole cloth by Wesley, promoted for centuries to come standards of beauty that privileged the philosophical, literary, and artistic output of white, male western Europeans.

40. Ibid., 467.

41. Ibid.

told. Yet it was Charles who was the first to attempt the experiment of "holy living" while a student at Oxford with his brother; it was Charles who first underwent a dramatic conversion experience in his early thirties; and it was Charles who penned these well-known lines about that life-altering event:

> And can it be, that I should gain
> An interest in the Saviour's blood?
> Died he for me, who caused his pain?
> For me? Who him to death pursued?
> Amazing love! How can it be
> That Thou, my God, shouldst die for me?[42]

From the beginning of the Methodist movement, Charles Wesley's hymns—he wrote more than six thousand over the course of his life—were its musical accompaniment. And while John Wesley's treatises, tracts, and sermons form the core of official Methodist doctrine (and have from the earliest decades), it is the hymns of Charles that have had the "greater influence on the identity and sense of community experienced by members of Methodist churches."[43] Lifelong Methodists know, for instance, that "O For a Thousand Tongues to Sing" is the denomination's signature anthem and has been the opening hymn in every Methodist hymnbook since the 1780 *Collection of Hymns for the Use of the People Called Methodists*. And even beyond Methodism, hymns like "Christ the Lord is Risen Today" and "Hark! the Herald Angels Sing" continue to resonate with worshipers across a range of ecclesial traditions.

Charles Wesley's hymns are rooted in Scripture, of course, and in his own experience, but he also drew widely on classic Latin texts, English poetry, patristic writings, and church doctrine. Moreover, he did not hesitate, as theologian Teresa Berger has noted, "to use his hymns as weapons in a variety of theological skirmishes, which would break out from time to time within the renewal movement."[44] For example, protests against Quietism—a Moravian practice of stillness before God and a refraining from acts of devotion and service until perfect faith was attained—found their way into several hymns published not long after Charles's conversion experience. And not long after that, he took to task the predestination of

---

42. "And Can It Be," quoted in Berger, *Theology in Hymns*, 64.

43. Ibid., 66.

44. Ibid., 106.

George Whitefield, a fellow revivalist with whom he and John had a long and stormy relationship.[45]

Berger's important study delves deeply into the hymnody of Charles Wesley, examining especially how the language of praise and adoration is intimately related to doctrine and theology. She notes the prominent themes of Wesley's work: salvation (including God's will for universal salvation), the nature of revelation, eschatology, and Christian perfection. Berger contends that for Charles Wesley, everything comes together in the experience of salvation: the beginning of eternal life, happiness, and heaven on earth.[46] The doctrine of Christian perfection is inextricably linked to salvation since the latter is understood to include and culminate in God's ongoing, sanctifying work in the lives of the faithful. In the Wesleyan lexicon, "entire sanctification" is a synonym for Christian perfection. The 1780 *Collection* attests to this Wesleyan distinctive in that it "contains two large sections of hymns devoted to the struggle for Christian perfection that when taken together comprise a greater number of hymns than any other section."[47]

The word "struggle" here is instructive. First, because it indicates the difficulty—the impossibility, we might insist—of human beings attaining something called perfection, and second, because the Wesleys themselves, and all the early adherents to Methodism, struggled to find agreement on what such an idea really meant—what perfection might look like practically, materially in the day-to-day lives of followers of Jesus.

John Wesley knew what he was up against simply in raising the subject: "There is scarce any expression in Holy Writ which has given more offence than this. The word *perfect* is what many cannot bear. The very sound of it is an abomination to them. And whosoever preaches perfection (as the phrase is)—that is, asserts that it is attainable in this life—runs great hazard of being accounted by them worse than a heathen man or a publican."[48] Both John and Charles were convinced of the truth of Christian perfection: the freedom from sin that belongs to those who are justified by Christ's saving work. Yet their individual views—especially those of Charles—would shift over the course of their lives and they would never

45. From a poem of ten stanzas, published in *Hymns on God's Everlasting Love* (1741), quoted in Berger, *Theology in Hymns*, 108–9: "O for a trumpet-voice / On all the world to call, / To bid their hearts rejoice / In him who died for all! / For all my Lord was crucified / For all, for all my Saviour died!"

46. Berger, *Theology in Hymns*, 138.

47. Ibid., 144.

48. Wesley, "Christian Perfection."

quite see eye to eye on how this doctrine is lived and practiced. Following his conversion experience in Aldersgate, John began to preach, controversially, that "justifying faith would bring instantaneous moral perfection, manifest in consummate affections and sinless actions (although involuntary 'infirmities' would remain)."[49] Soon thereafter, however, he would adjust his views—overcorrecting in such a way that he courted even more controversy, positing a distinction between "new birth" in Christ and a later time of being born of God "in the full sense." In this latter stage, God's grace would instantly free the believer from all sin—"not only sinful actions, but also corrupt tempers, evil thoughts, and even temptations!"[50] John would continue to modify his views in response to criticism, much of it virulent, insisting in his later years that Christian perfection is not necessary for salvation. But "to the end of his ministry he would exhort his followers to 'go on to perfection,' as something they could attain *now*."[51]

Charles's hymns on Christian perfection draw frequently and explicitly on passages from across the New Testament. Reflecting on 1 Thess 4:3, he wrote these lines in an early hymn:

> He wills that I should holy be:
> What can withstand his will?[52]

When members of the Methodist movement began professing perfection for themselves, raising concerns for Charles that such presumption surely falsified their claims, he continued to maintain that sinlessness in one's lifetime was attainable. (Such was the pull of Scripture literally understood by the eighteenth-century enthusiasts). Over time, however, empirical evidence won out, and Charles "relegated his concept of Christian perfection to eschatological categories and began to associate the attainment of Christian perfection with the death of the believer."[53] This was in tension, of course, with John's belief that perfection was possible during one's lifetime, even if it was not a given or a requirement for the fullness of salvation in the lives of the faithful. "The difference between the brothers on this issue," Berger notes, "would lead John in some instances to criticize his brother's

49. Maddox, *Responsible Grace*, 181.

50. Wesley, preface to the 1740 edition of *Hymns and Sacred Poems*, quoted in Maddox, *Responsible Grace*, 181.

51. Maddox, *Responsible Grace*, 186. Maddox's italics.

52. Wesley, *Collection of Hymns*, quoted in Berger, *Theology in Hymns*, 143.

53. Berger, *Theology in Hymns*, 143.

hymns on Christian perfection, marking them in the margins, even editing out hymn stanzas and lines that did not coincide with his own view."[54]

For Charles, the shift to understanding Christian perfection as a state of being yet to come was accompanied by an evolving theological conviction: that attainment of perfection (even in death) is not due to the believer's strivings for sinlessness but to God's re-creating work.

> The thing my God doth hate,
> That I no more may do,
> Thy creature, Lord, again create,
> And all my soul renew;
> My soul shall then, like thine,
> Abhor the thing unclean,
> And sanctified by love divine
> Forever cease from sin.[55]

Charles incorporated in his hymns two interrelated motifs to signal this shift in perspective: Christian perfection as a restoration of the *imago Dei* and as a recovery of Eden:

> Father, Son, and Holy Ghost,
> Be to us what Adam lost;
> Let us in thine image rise,
> Give us back our paradise![56]

Moreover, the form of these poetic lines is almost always that of petition:

> Let us, to perfect love restored,
> Thy image here receive.[57]

And again:

> Stamp thine image on my heart.[58]

Berger notes that in presenting these themes in the language of prayer, Charles "reinforces the notion that Christian perfection is granted by God to humankind"; it is not something achieved by the individual, and it is

54. Ibid., 143–44.
55. Wesley, *Collection of Hymns*, 487.
56. Ibid., 689.
57. Ibid., 489.
58. Ibid., 557.

always *anticipated*. "Nowhere in his hymns does Charles Wesley look back and give thanks for the gift of Christian perfection."[59]

One last image employed by Charles in his hymns on Christian perfection helps us begin to see the contours of a theology of beauty in Wesleyan doctrine. In the slow shift from considering perfection a moral achievement to naming it divine gift, Charles drew on another New Testament letter—a passage in 2 Peter that speaks of the promise of becoming "participants in the divine nature" (1:4). While Charles's later views on Christian perfection emphasize the restoration of the image of God in the believer and recovering the divine-human relationship of Eden, it also includes—is of a piece with, in fact—sharing in the very life of God:

> Send us the Spirit of thy Son
> To make the depths of Godhead known,
> To make us share the life divine;
> Send him the sprinkled blood t'apply,
> Send him our souls to sanctify,
> And show and seal us ever thine.[60]

And in another hymn, these lines:

> The promise stands forever sure,
> And we shall in thine image shine,
> Partakers of a nature pure,
> Holy, angelical, divine;
> In spirit joined to thee the Son,
> As thou art with thy Father one.[61]

Here Christian perfection names that state of being for which humans were created: communion with God. And since God's nature is that of love, to participate in the divine nature is to share in the perfect love that is God's very being. Augustine believed that we are made beautiful when we love, and here, similarly, the ethical impulse of much of the early Wesleyan doctrine of perfection (the striving to be good) is subsumed into (or overridden by) an aesthetic one since the goal is not perfect living but perfect loving. And if God's love is God's beauty (and also God's truth and goodness), then John and Charles Wesley gave shape to a doctrine of perfection

---

59. Berger, *Theology in Hymns*, 147.

60. Wesley, *Collection of Hymns*, 536.

61. Ibid., 369:8.

that acknowledges divine beauty and our participation in it and our witness to it: "The beauty of holiness, of that inward man of the heart which is renewed after the image of God, cannot but strike every eye which God hath opened, every enlightened understanding."[62] We see also how perfect love as a life of beauty is linked to happiness and to health: "Whatever ye desire or fear, whatever ye seek or shun, whatever ye think, speak, or do, be it in order to your happiness in God, the sole end, as well as source, of your being."[63]

So long as Christian perfection is framed ethically as a striving toward sinlessness, the failure to achieve it is obvious. But conceived aesthetically, Christian perfection names that "loving consent toward the other" that characterizes the divine beauty in which we partake.[64] Expressed, embodied, and borne witness to, this beauty-as-lived-practice takes many forms.

A Beautiful Life

Beauty is communicative. A work of art, for example, is the expressed form that makes the beautiful visible. In the terms we have been exploring in this chapter, we could say that to be beautiful is to give visibility, substance, *form* to a foundational truth of our creatureliness. Beauty, we recall, is not "extra" to our nature as human beings. Rather, "part of what it means to be, is to be beautiful. Beauty is not superadded to things; it is one of the springs of their reality."[65] But how is it expressed, communicated, *made known*? Not as a general human sensitivity to beautiful things (though this is a desirable human trait). Instead, beauty reveals itself—as the Wesleyan doctrine of perfection suggests—as a "disposition to benevolence," as an active seeking of the well-being of all that exists.[66] Theologically put, it is Christ who gives visible form to the infinite, ineffable beauty of God, to the dramatic movement, the dance of divine love (*perichoresis*) of Father, Son, and Holy Spirit.[67] And Christ's beauty, as we have noted, is the beauty of an

---

62. Wesley, "Upon Our Lord's Sermon on the Mount, Discourse IV," in Wesley, *Works*, 1:531.

63. Wesley, "A Plain Account of Christian Perfection."

64. Vanhoozer, "Praising in Song," 117.

65. Murphy, *Christ the Form of Beauty*, 42.

66. Farley, *Faith and Beauty*, 45.

67. From the Greek *peri* (around) and *chorea* (dance). Early Christian theologians like Gregory of Nazianzus used this term to describe the harmony and intimacy that

action—of a life lived, of a humiliating death, of a conquering of the finality of death. Christ draws us into the beauty of the triune God and summons from us outward expressions of what we already are: sharers in the divine nature, bearers of the beauty of God. For the Wesleys this summons is best understood as Scripture's clear call to love God and our neighbor. And this, too, is the centerpiece of Christian perfection: "By perfection," John Wesley said, as he struggled again and again to communicate this doctrine clearly and cogently to his numerous critics, "I mean the humble, gentle, patient love of God, and our neighbour, ruling our tempers, words, and actions."[68]

To live a beautiful life, then, is to love as we are loved by God—freely, without strings or conditions; extravagantly, without counting the cost or keeping score; fully, with joyful abandon, holding nothing back. It is to be caught up in the drama of divine love and intimacy and mutuality and generosity. It is not merely an inner state. It is, as Francesca Murphy notes, "a thing done."[69] Here we can recall the story of the prodigal son recounted in chapter 1. As the prodigally wasteful son finds welcome and abundance and *home* in the prodigal love of the father, he is free to become a bearer of beauty, to love as he has been loved: extravagantly, joyfully, completely. Poet Christian Wiman puts it like this: "To manage this highest form of loving does not mean that we will be showered with earthly delights or somehow be spared awful human suffering. But for as long as we can live in this sacred space of receiving and releasing, and can learn to speak and be love's fluency, then the greater love that is God brings a continuous and enlarging air into our existence. We feel love leave us in unthreatening ways. We feel it reenter us at once more truly and more strange, like a simple kiss that has a bite of starlight in it."[70]

If Christ most perfectly exemplifies the beautiful, he does this even as, *only as*, he enters into human existence. From Augustine to Balthasar, the beauty of Christ is a crucified beauty. The ceaseless self-giving of Father, Son, and Holy Spirit, each to the other, was made manifest in the self-emptying of Christ on the cross in the face of first-century imperial power. And here we return to a question asked at the beginning of this chapter:

---

constitute the eternal relations of the Trinity. In Scripture, John 14 communicates something of this truth of God's being (and our share in it) when Jesus says, "I am in the Father, and you in me, and I in you" (v. 20).

68. Wesley, "Brief Thoughts on Christian Perfection."
69. Murphy, *Christ the Form of Beauty*, 18.
70. Wiman, *My Bright Abyss*, 24.

Where do we locate beauty in a world of radical evil? The human capacity for sin must surely in some way efface the beauty of our beingness, but to what degree? And how is it possible to live lives of beauty in the midst of the brokenness and diminishment that sin and evil, individually and collectively, bring about?

The church professes that the redemption accomplished by Jesus's life, death, and resurrection restores the divine image in all of creation. As the early church theologian Athanasius put it, the Word became flesh to reestablish the original pattern after which the human form was crafted in the beginning, and to impress upon creation anew the beauty of the divine image.[71] In Jesus's encounter with the powers and principalities, in his confrontation with the terrorist politics of Roman occupation and oppression, a reversal took place—the story of sin and evil and violence and death was retold. "In Christ," writes Hart, "a real and visible beauty has cast its light upon the figure of sinful humanity and revealed it to be a false image, an apostasy of the soul from its own beauty."[72] Hart goes on to say, "Christ's moment of most absolute particularity—the absolute dereliction of the cross—is the moment in which the glory of God, his power to be where and when he will be, is displayed before the eyes of the world."[73]

This is the crucified beauty of Christ that his body, the church, bears witness to as it seeks to open itself to the gift of being made beautiful for God and for the world. And yet this is an undertaking fraught with risk. As Hart notes, "Even in the strength of the Spirit there is a terrible fragility to the beauty that the form of Christ restores to creation, because it can be imparted only as a gift, which may be rejected."[74] One saving hope in this work of living beautifully is to understand its social dimension—that to bear the *imago Dei* is to be in relationship with God, other persons, all of creation. Theologically speaking, we are not individuals who happen to forge or fashion or stumble upon connections to others. Rather, personhood is constituted communally such that we are bound by our very beingness one to another. Another way of saying this, as Francesca Murphy observes, is that Christ's saving work "binds historical community into himself."[75] The beautiful life is *received* and then *returned* in acts of love to the neighbor,

71. Athanasius, *De incarnatione* 11–16; see Hart, *Beauty of the Infinite*, 325.

72. Hart, *Beauty of the Infinite*, 326.

73. Ibid., 327.

74. Ibid., 339.

75. Murphy, *Christ the Form of Beauty*, 184.

the stranger, the enemy—acts that mirror the self-emptying love of Jesus and the extravagant generosity of our prodigal God.

↭

In his book *Something Beautiful for God,* English journalist Malcolm Muggeridge makes this observation about Mother Teresa—a woman he found to be "less sentimental, less scatty, more down-to-earth" than anyone he had ever met:

> When the train began to move, and I walked away, I felt as though I were leaving behind me all the beauty and all the joy in the universe. Something of God's universal love has rubbed off on Mother Teresa, giving her homely features a noticeable luminosity; a shining quality. She has lived as closely with her Lord that the same enchantment clings about her that sent the crowds chasing after him in Jerusalem and Galilee, and made his mere presence seem a harbinger of healing. Outside, the streets were beginning to stir; sleepers awakening, stretching and yawning; some raking over the piles of garbage in search of something edible. It was a scene of desolation, yet it, too, seemed somehow irradiated. This love, this Christian love, which shines down on the misery we make, and into our dark hearts that make it; irradiating all, uniting all, making of all one stupendous harmony. Momentarily I understood; then, leaning back in my American limousine, was carried off to breakfast, to pick over my own particular garbage-heap.[76]

Summary

In chapter 1 we drew on the gospel story of the woman who anoints Jesus with costly perfume. When the astonished and offended onlookers make known their indignation, Jesus quiets them with these words: "Why do you trouble her? She has done a beautiful thing for me" (Mark 14:6; Matt 26:10 ESV). In her singular gesture, her wordless love, this unnamed woman makes beauty visible. In an undertaking fraught with risk she returns what she had been given: prodigal love freely poured out—no counting the cost, nothing held back. She, like Mother Teresa and countless others known and unknown, bears the beauty of the divine image in self-emptying action, in

---

76. Muggeridge, *Something Beautiful for God,* 17–18.

mission for the sake of the world. For all that seems extraordinary about this tender act, it offers for us a witness, a model for how we, too, in ordinary, everyday ways might learn to be possessed by beauty, to open our lives, individually and corporately, to the gift, the call, the joyful art of becoming beautiful.

Questions for Consideration

1. What are the ways in which we may consider doctrine beautiful? Ugly? Explain.

2. What is the purpose of doctrine in the life of the church?

3. What is the relationship between doctrine and pedagogy (teaching and learning) and worship?

4. What is the doctrine of beauty? What is beauty?

   a. How is beauty woven into the very being and character of God, the Christian life, the church?

   b. Why has beauty been so overlooked as a matter of theological reflection, from creation to crucifixion to discipleship, in the modern era? What is the consequence of this oversight, and how has it contributed to utilitarian forms of thinking, or ways of avoiding true happiness? What is the connection between beauty and happiness?

5. How is the Christian life itself beautiful?

   a. What are the ways in which we may understand beauty as something we do not possess but as that which possesses us?

   b. What role did the Protestant Reformers play in the devaluation of beauty? Is it a contradiction to speak of a Protestant aesthetic? Explain.

6. What is a Wesleyan understanding of beauty?

   a. How does John Wesley's view that art occupies a plane of existence distinct from vital piety keep beauty and the Christian life separate?

   b. How, in Wesley's eyes, may art serve as a "handmaid of piety"? Explain both positive and negative aspects of this insight.

   c. How is Wesley's understanding of beauty in keeping with the long line of Enlightenment thinkers, and how may such an understanding fail to see what beauty is?

7. What is the relationship between Wesley's doctrine of perfection and beauty?

   a. Share some of the tensions in the Wesleyan understanding of Christian perfection.

   b. How might Charles Wesley's themes of Christian perfection in his hymns provide a picture of life in God, not as achievement but as gift?

   c. How are such themes of perfect love related to beauty, to God's truth and goodness, to happiness, to health, to being in communion with others?

8. What is the beautiful life and how is it intrinsically a foundational truth of our humanity?

   a. What does it mean in Wesleyan terms to live a beautiful life, as an answer to the call to share in God's own beauty or love?

   b. How does Jesus Christ on the cross exemplify the very beauty of God and how is such "crucified beauty" counter to modern notions of beauty?

   c. What makes it possible to live beautiful lives, as depicted from Augustine to Wesley to Balthasar? Based on the previous two chapters, what are the key aspects of producing and living and enjoying such lives?

   d. What are the risks we are to take in living lives of beauty?

9. Based on the above commentary and reflection, what "beautiful things" still await our lives together? What practices are necessary to cultivate such beauty in our respective communities and traditions? Where do we begin?

Afterword

I began writing this book while on an extended retreat at St. Meinrad Arch-abbey in southern Indiana. When you pray five times a day in a Benedictine community—with the arresting beauty of the liturgy, the patient pace of the psalmody, the lush silences—it is easy to forget that monasticism began as a protest movement in the midst of political chaos and decay. It is the *gentleness* of praying the liturgy of the hours that perhaps moves me most— the unhurried attentiveness, the graceful cadences of sung or spoken lines, the ceremonial courtesy one must show to those with whom one prays. (Whether or not one *feels* particularly amicable seems beside the point.) We live in the midst of a good deal of muscular Christianity—of stridency and bombast, of desperation for edginess and novelty and *noise*. And of course we live in a culture of violence and speed in which gentleness seems quaint, obsolete, irresponsible.

I mention all of this because St. Meinrad offered a rich setting for be-ginning my exploration of happiness, health, and beauty as ways to name the "everydayness" of the Christian life. My thinking about these matters was deeply enhanced by encounters there with men and women who de-sired to learn more of what it means to flourish together in the goodness of God (happiness), who cared about the intrinsic connection between bread and bodies (health), and who bore witness in mostly quiet, gentle ways to a "disposition to benevolence" that is the hallmark of our being fully human (beauty).

In the weeks of writing after my retreat, it was the gift of friendship that sustained the work. I am grateful for the encouragement of friends and family, students and colleagues. A special debt of gratitude is owed to those who took the time and care to read, reflect on, and respond to parts or all of the manuscript at its various stages: Alison Anderson, Nola Boezeman, Victor Hinojosa, Philip Kenneson, and Drew Murphy. Andy Kinsey's questions at the end of each chapter make this book eminently more useful than it otherwise would be. To him, to all the editors of this series, and to Charlie Collier and Jacob Martin at Cascade Books: my heartfelt thanks.

During the writing of this book I made the long-contemplated journey from lifelong Methodism to reception into the Roman Catholic Church. As this book series seeks to supplement the Wesleyan tradition with the gifts of the church catholic, the writing of this volume was regularly (and I hope fruitfully) informed by my traversing these two ecclesial traditions. It is my hope that this modest volume in this important series contributes in some small way to the unity and catholicity of Christ's body, the Church.

Bibliography

Alison, James. *The Joy of Being Wrong: Original Sin through Easter Eyes*. New York: Crossroad, 1998.

Allison, Dale C., Jr. *Studies in Matthew: Interpretation Past and Present*. Grand Rapids: Baker Academic, 2005.

Bahnson, Fred, and Norman Wirzba. *Making Peace with the Land: God's Call to Reconcile with Creation*. Downers Grove, IL: InterVarsity, 2012.

Balthasar, Hans Urs von. *The Glory of the Lord: A Theological Aesthetics*. Vol. 1, *Seeing the Form*. Translated by Erasmo Leiva-Merikakis. Edited by Joseph Fessio and John Riches. San Francisco: Ignatius, 1982.

———. *The Glory of the Lord: A Theological Aesthetics*. Vol. 5, *The Realm of Metaphysics in Antiquity*. Translated by Oliver Davies et al. Edited by Brian McNeil and John Riches. San Francisco: Ignatius, 1991.

———. "Transcendentality and Gestalt." *Communio* 11 (1984) 19–39.

Barth, Karl. *Church Dogmatics* II/1. Translated by G. W. Bromley and T. F. Torrance. Edinburgh: T. & T. Clark, 1957.

Bartholomew, Craig G., et al. *Reading Luke: Interpretation, Reflection, Formation*. Grand Rapids: Zondervan, 2005.

Begbie, Jeremy. "Beauty and Sentimentality in the Arts." In *The Beauty of God: Theology and the Arts*, edited by D. J. Treier et al., 45–69. Downers Grove, IL: InterVarsity, 2007.

———. "Created Beauty: The Witness of J. S. Bach." In *The Beauty of God: Theology and the Arts*, edited by D. J. Treier et al., 19–44. Downers Grove, IL: InterVarsity, 2007.

Benedict XVI, Pope. Homily for the Solemnity of the Sacred Heart of Jesus. St. Peter's Basilica, June 19, 2009. http://www.vatican.va/holy_father/benedict_xvi/homilies/2009/documents/hf_ben-xvi_hom_20090619_anno-sac_en.html.

Berger, Teresa. *Theology in Hymns: A Study of the Relationship of Doxology and Theology according to* A Collection of Hymns for the Use of the People Called Methodists (1780). Nashville: Kingswood, 1995.

Berry, Wendell. "Health Is Membership." In *Another Turn of the Crank*, 86–112. Berkeley: Counterpoint, 1995.

———. "The Pleasures of Eating." In *What Are People For?*, 145–52. San Francisco: North Point, 1990.

Boehm, Julia K., and Laura D. Kubzansky. "The Heart's Content: The Association between Positive Psychological Well-Being and Cardiovascular Health." *Psychological Bulletin* 138 (2012) 655–91.

Bonhoeffer, Dietrich. *Discipleship.* Edited by Geffrey B. Kelly and John D. Godsey. Translated by Barbara Green and Reinhard Krauss. Dietrich Bonhoeffer Works 4. Minneapolis: Fortress, 2001.

———. *Ethics.* Edited by Clifford J. Green. Translated by Reinhard Krauss et al. Dietrich Bonhoeffer Works 6. Minneapolis: Fortress, 2005.

Bretherton, Luke. *Christianity and Contemporary Politics: The Conditions and Possibilities of Faithful Witness.* Oxford: Blackwell, 2009.

Bruner, Frederick Dale. *Matthew, The Christbook: Matthew 1–12.* Grand Rapids: Eerdmans, 2004.

Buechner, Frederick. *Wishful Thinking: A Seeker's ABC.* San Francisco: HarperOne, 1993.

Calvin, John. *The Institutes of the Christian Religion.* Translated by Henry Beveridge. Reprint, Peabody, MA: Hendrickson, 2008.

Capon, Robert Farrar. *The Supper of the Lamb: A Culinary Reflection.* Garden City, NY: Doubleday, 1969.

Cavanaugh, William T. *Being Consumed: Economics and Christian Desire.* Grand Rapids: Eerdmans, 2008.

Ciardi, John. "Is Everybody Happy?" *Saturday Review*, March 14, 1964, 18–20.

Coles, Robert. *Dorothy Day: A Radical Devotion.* Cambridge: Da Capo, 1989.

Coogan, Michael D. "Salvation." In *The Oxford Companion to the Bible*, edited by Bruce M. Metzger and Michael D. Coogan, 669–70. New York: Oxford University Press, 1993.

David, Hans T., and Arthur Mendel, eds. *The Bach Reader: A Life of Johann Sebastian Bach in Letters and Documents.* New York: Norton, 1966.

De Gruchy, John. "Holy Beauty: A Reformed Perpsective on Aesthetics in a World of Ugly Injustice." In *Reformed Theology for the Third Christian Millenium: The 2001 Sprunt Lectures*, edited by Brian Gerrish, 13–25. Louisville: Westminster John Knox, 2003.

Dinesen, Isak. *Babette's Feast and Other Anecdotes of Destiny.* New York: Vintage, 1988.

Edwards, Jonathan. *Religious Affections.* Edited by John E. Smith. Works of Jonathan Edwards 2. New Haven: Yale University Press, 1959.

Farley, Edward. *Faith and Beauty: A Theological Aesthetic.* Aldershot, UK: Ashgate, 2001.

Gregory of Nyssa. *Homilies on the Beatitudes: An English Version with Commentary and Supporting Studies.* Edited by Hubertus R. Drobner and Alberto Viciano. Boston: Brill, 2000.

Hart, David Bentley. *The Beauty of the Infinite: The Aesthetics of Christian Truth.* Grand Rapids: Ecrdmans, 2004.

Hauerwas, Stanley. *Matthew.* Brazos Theological Commentary on the Bible. Grand Rapids: Brazos, 2006.

Hauerwas, Stanley, and Jean Vanier. *Living Gently in a Violent World: The Prophetic Witness of Weakness.* Downers Grove, IL: InterVarsity, 2008.

Hays, Richard. *The Moral Vision of the New Testament—Community, Cross, New Community: A Contemporary Introduction to New Testament Ethics.* San Francisco: Harper, 1996.

Howell, James. *The Beatitudes for Today.* Louisville: Westminster John Knox, 2005.

Kierkegaard, Søren. *Purity of Heart Is to Will One Thing.* Translated by Douglas V. Steere. Lexington: Feather Trail, 2009.

Lane, Belden. "Jonathan Edwards on Beauty, Desire, and the Sensory World." *Theological Studies* 65 (2004) 44–72.

Lee, Sang Hyun. *The Philosophical Theology of Jonathan Edwards*. Princeton: Princeton University Press, 1988.

Levertov, Denise. *Breathing the Water*. New York: New Directions, 1987.

Maddox, Randy. *Responsible Grace: John Wesley's Practical Theology*. Nashville: Abingdon, 1994.

McCabe, Herbert. *The Good Life: Ethics and the Pursuit of Happiness*. New York: Continuum, 2005.

McDermott, Gerald R. *Understanding Jonathan Edwards: An Introduction to America's Theologian*. Oxford: Oxford University Press, 2008.

Miles, Sara. *Take This Bread: A Radical Conversion*. New York: Ballantine, 2007.

Mitchell, Louis J. *Jonathan Edwards on the Experience of Beauty*. Studies in Reformed Theology and History, New Series, 9. Princeton: Princeton Theological Seminary, 2003.

Mounce, Robert H. *Matthew*. Peabody, MA: Hendrickson, 1991.

Muggeridge, Malcolm. *Something Beautiful for God*. New York: Harper and Row, 1971.

Murphy, Debra Dean. "'Beautiful and Pointless': Poetry and the Theological Task." In *From Each Brave Eye: Reflections on the Arts, Ministry, and Holy Imagination*, edited by Todd Edmondson. eBook. Colorado Springs: Shook Foil, 2013.

———. *Teaching That Transforms: Worship as the Heart of Christian Education*. Grand Rapids: Brazos, 2004.

Murphy, Francesca Aran. *Christ the Form of Beauty: A Study in Theology and Literature*. Edinburgh: T. & T. Clark, 1995.

Niebuhr, Reinhold. *An Interpretation of Christian Ethics*. New York: Seabury, 1979.

Nouwen, Henri. *The Return of the Prodigal Son: A Story of Homecoming*. London: Darton, Longman and Todd, 1994.

Oden, Thomas C. *Doctrinal Standards in the Wesleyan Tradition*. Nashville: Abingdon, 1988.

Petrini, Carlo. *Slow Food Nation: The Creation of a New Gastronomy*. New York: Rizzoli, 2007.

Petrini, Carlo, and Gigi Padovani. *Slow Food Revolution: A New Culture for Eating and Living*. New York: Rizzoli, 2006.

Pollan, Michael. *Food Rules: An Eater's Manual*. New York: Penguin, 2009.

Preston, Geoffrey. *God's Way to Be Man*. London: Darton, Longman and Todd, 1978.

Radcliffe, Timothy. *Why Go to Church? The Drama of the Eucharist*. New York: Continuum, 2008.

Rattenbury, J. Ernest. *The Eucharistic Hymns of John and Charles Wesley*. Nashville: Abingdon, 1947.

———. *The Eucharistic Hymns of John and Charles Wesley*. American ed. Edited by T. Crouch. Akron, OH: Order of St. Luke, 1996.

Robinson, Marilynne. *Gilead*. New York: Farrar, Straus and Giroux, 2004.

Rogal, Samuel J. "Pills for the Pill: John Wesley's *Primitive Physick*." *The Yale Journal of Biology and Medicine* 51 (1978) 81–90.

Romero, Óscar. *The Violence of Love*. Compiled and translated by James R. Brockman. Maryknoll, NY: Orbis, 2004.

Routley, Erik. *The Musical Wesleys, 1703–1876*. New York: Oxford University Press, 1968.

Sauvage, Pierre. *Weapons of the Spirit*. Pierre Sauvage Productions, 1989.

Scheper-Hughes, Nancy. *Death without Weeping: The Violence of Everyday Life in Brazil*. Berkeley: University of California Press, 1992.

Schmemann, Alexander. *For the Life of the World: Sacraments and Orthodoxy.* Crestwood, NY: St. Vladimir's Seminary Press, 1973.

Senn, Frank C. *Christian Liturgy: Catholic and Evangelical.* Minneapolis: Fortress, 1997.

Sherry, Patrick. *Spirit and Beauty: An Introduction to Theological Aesthetics.* 2nd ed. London: SCM, 2002.

Stevens, Rosemary. *Medical Practice in Modern England: The Impact of Specialization and State Medicine.* New Haven: Yale University Press, 1966.

Thomas, Aquinas. *Summa Theologiae.* Translated by Thomas Gilby. New York: McGraw-Hill, 1969.

Tyson, Timothy B. *Blood Done Sign My Name.* New York: Crown, 2004.

Vanhoozer, Kevin J. "Praising in Song: Beauty and the Arts." In *The Blackwell Companion to Christian Ethics*, edited by Stanley Hauerwas and Samuel Wells, 110–22. Oxford: Blackwell, 2004.

Wadell, Paul. *Happiness and the Christian Moral Life: An Introduction to Christian Ethics.* Lanham, MD: Rowman and Littlefield, 2012.

Wells, Samuel. *Learning to Dream Again: Rediscovering the Heart of God.* Grand Rapids: Eerdmans, 2013.

Wesley, John. "Brief Thoughts in Christian Perfection." http://gbgm-umc.org/umhistory/wesley/perfect8.html.

———. "Christian Perfection." The Wesley Center Online. http://wesley.nnu.edu/john-wesley/the-sermons-of-john-wesley-1872-edition/sermon-40-christian-perfection/.

———. *A Collection of Hymns for the Use of the People Called Methodists.* London: J. Paramore, 1780.

———. "The Duty of Constant Communion." The Wesley Center Online. http://wesley.nnu.edu/john-wesley/the-sermons-of-john-wesley-1872-edition/sermon-101-the-duty-of-constant-communion/.

———. *The Hymnbook: A Collection of Hymns for the Use of People Called Methodists.* Edited by Franz Hildebrandt and Oliver A. Beckerlegge. Works of John Wesley 7. Oxford: Clarendon, 1983.

———. *The Journal of the Rev. John Wesley.* Edited by Nehemiah Curnock. 8 vols. London: Epworth, 1938.

———. "A Plain Account of Christian Perfection." The Wesley Center Online. http://wesley.nnu.edu/john-wesley/a-plain-account-of-christian-perfection/.

———. *Primitive Physick: Or, an Easy and Natural Method of Curing Most Diseases.* 1786. Reprint, Eugene, OR: Wipf and Stock, 2003.

———. "Rules of the Band Societies: Drawn Up Dec. 25, 1738." In vol. 9 of *The Works of John Wesley*, edited by Rupert E. Davies, 77–79. Nashville: Abingdon, 1989.

———. "Thoughts Upon Taste." In vol. 13 of *The Works of the Rev. John Wesley: With the Last Corrections of the Author.* Google eBook.

———. "The Unity of Divine Being." The Wesley Center Online. http://wesley.nnu.edu/john-wesley/the-sermons-of-john-wesley-1872-edition/sermon-114-the-unity-of-the-divine-being/.

———. *The Works of John Wesley.* Vol. 1., *Sermons I, 1–33.* Edited by Albert C. Outler. Nashville: Abingdon, 1984.

Whelan, Matthew. "The Responsible Body: A Eucharistic Community." *Cross Currents* 51.3 (2001). http://www.crosscurrents.org/whelan.htm.

Williams, Colin. *John Wesley's Theology Today.* Nashville: Abingdon, 1960.

Wiman, Christian. *My Bright Abyss: Meditation of a Modern Believer.* New York: Farrar, Straus and Giroux, 2013.

Wink, Walter. *The Powers That Be: Theology for a New Millennium.* New York: Random House, 1999.

Wright, N. T. *Surprised by Hope: Rethinking Heaven, Resurrection, and the Mission of the Church.* New York: HarperCollins, 2008.

Printed in Great Britain
by Amazon

56304476R00066